MANAGING
By the Numbers

MANAGING
By the Numbers

Financial Essentials
for the Growing Business

David H. Bangs, Jr.

Upstart Publishing Company
Dover, New Hampshire

To my friend Roger Parker, writer, artist and lunch companion, for his many thoughtful ideas on how to run businesses—and his almost total aversion to managing by the numbers. The world of business presents many ways to succeed, and Roger continually astounds me. Most of all, he understands the weird pressures that make writers moody, and helps me get through to the deadlines. Thanks, Roger! Let's go sailing.

Published by:
Upstart Publishing Company, Inc.
A Division of Dearborn Publishing Group, Inc.
12 Portland Street
Dover, New Hampshire 03820
(603) 749-5071

ISBN: 0-936894-26-1

For a complete catalog of Upstart publications, call 1-800-235-8866.

Contents

Foreword

I wrote *Managing by the Numbers* to help small-business owners take advantage of the information generated by their businesses. Some owners, the successful ones, recognize the importance of gathering and organizing information to simplify their day-to-day managerial tasks.

Other owners rarely look at the numbers and then only for a limited set of reasons: Their bankers request up-to-date financials or ask embarrassing questions about the financial structure of the business. The Internal Revenue Service demands certain financial information. Vendors ask for financial information so they can establish credit worthiness. A prospective buyer of the business performing "due diligence" asks for financials to help put a value on it.

These are all legitimate reasons for heeding the numbers, but the most important reason for a serious business owner to seek out and understand financial and other measures is that it helps keep the business under control, purposeful, focused on goals that make sense for that business.

Your business plan provides an overview of the business, a set of financial projections (both budgets and operating plans) based on the resources available, goals that are in line with current economic conditions and a financing plan to satisfy the most cynical banker.

The financial statements contained in your business plan provide the basis for managing by the numbers. The projected profit & loss statement (also called the income statement), cash flow *pro forma* and balance sheet embody your business goals over one to three years. (Longer time frames are inappropriate. Unlike large businesses, small enterprises don't have sufficient assets, market presence and momentum to look forward several years with even spurious accuracy.)

The essence of managing by the numbers is easy to state: measure actual performance against standards. This sounds simple enough. But in practice managing by the numbers is complex and requires close attention to a number of subtly interwoven notions.

Prime among these is discipline. Managing by the numbers is useless if not consistently and carefully applied. It is based on measuring progress against pre-established goals. Managing by the numbers is proactive management. The more common method is to react to whatever is currently pressing.

Managing by the numbers is goal-oriented and so avoids short-term shifts. This is a more professional method of management than most small business owners are used to. Yet it is stunningly simple. Set goals, measure progress toward them and reap the profits.

Managing by the numbers lacks the excitement of fire fighting. It is not a quick cure. Managing by the numbers calls for patience. It will, over time, simplify running the business and help you prevent brushfires, especially if used in conjunction with your business plan.

Establishing goals and standards is the trickiest part of managing by the numbers. You have to know what standards to use for measuring your business. The two categories of goals are external, based on trade or industry data, and internal, generated from historical and projected performance of the business. Not surprisingly, there is a close relationship between these standards. Historical performance is an excellent first approximation to the immediate future, unless substantial changes in the market (due to competition, economic factors or your plans for your business) are anticipated. In this latter case, historical performance is a powerful modifier of any changes. Your business has an economic and market momentum that is difficult to change radically.

You use external standards as a check on how realistic your projected internal standards are. The tension between internal and external standards illuminates and explicates such areas as capital needs, growth limitations, credit and collection practices and a host of other vital areas. The external standards establish outer limits; the internal standards work within these limits. If they fall outside them, warning flags go up. Trade and industry data, while not perfect, are based on many businesses' performance. Some of this data is compiled from tax returns. Some comes from banks and accounting firms, but most trade data come from businesses with an interest in comparing themselves to similar businesses.

Since there are some 22,000 trade associations in the U.S. alone, the chances of locating trade information are high. The editors of trade magazines are always interested in securing financial data because it sells magazines. Trade association executives are interested in numbers for recruiting and retaining members. The information is there, though you may have to dig for it.

Less specific compilations of financial data, such as the Robert Morris Associates' *Annual Statement Studies* (RMA) or Financial Research Associates' *Financial Statement Studies of the Small Business* (FMA), are found in most libraries with business interests. Bankers swear by the RMA, though the relevance of their figures to smaller enterprises or start-ups is strained. They do provide a framework to compare businesses and should be part of your arsenal if only to help you disarm questions your banker may raise. The FRA figures are better for small businesses, but are limited in the numbers of businesses covered.

Your business' past performance provides a basis for discerning trends. Much of Managing by the numbers is based on trend analysis. Trends highlight important though hard-to-see shifts in how you do business. Isolated numbers are less interesting from a managing by the numbers view than a series of numbers which indicate a pattern or trend.

Finally, internally established goals, based on your plans and moderated by economic conditions, must be observed in context. If market or economic conditions change dramatically, reassess your goals. How often? I'd suggest quarterly revisions, but only if needed. Due to the prevalence of computers, revising goals and expressing them in measurable numbers is not such a chore as it once was.

Hidden in this discussion are some important non-financial or quasi-financial numbers. These are just as important to the success of your company as the figures on the P & L. For example, how many sales calls does or should your sales force make each week? How do you keep track of actual sales calls so you can keep sales growing?

Managing by the numbers is a powerful tool. This book puts it at your disposal. It's up to you to adapt it to your own business.

David H. Bangs, Jr.
Portsmouth, New Hampshire
January 1, 1992

Acknowledgments

Part I, Company-wide Measures, was strongly influenced by Bob Brinson and his Halcyon Group. With his approval and encouragement, I have paraphrased and quoted from Halcyon's copyrighted material, especially their booklet entitled "Profiting from Financial Statements." The chapter on strategic analysis is especially indebted to Halcyon; it uses their example and much of their initial explanation.

The Halcyon Group developed and sells an excellent computerized financial management system, "fisCAL™ Business Analysis System," which makes some financial tools much more available to small-business owners than has been possible in the past.

fisCAL™ contains current Robert Morris Associates' and Financial Research Associates' comparative financial data. This inclusion sets Halcyon's project apart from competing computer-based financial programs. This wealth of computerized financial data greatly simplifies the comparison of one business (such as yours) with other businesses.

You can get ordering and other information on fisCAL™ from

    Robert J. Brinson
    The Halcyon Group Inc.
    449 Fleming Road
    Charleston, SC 29412–9904
    Tel: 803–795–7336

Other particularly helpful friends and colleagues include Brian Knight and Country Business Inc., John Blackford, Henry Villaume, Tom Weber, Ed Kearney, Bill Eldridge, and the dozens of small-business owners, led by Mike Goslin of Finestkind Seafoods in York ME, who have patiently allowed me to inflict my ideas on them over the years.

What is "Managing by the Numbers"?

If you can measure an activity, you can control it and improve performance. Whether it is company-wide ("Did we make a profit?") or individual ("You exceeded quota by the end of the third week. Well done!"), the concept is the same. In managing by the numbers you periodically measure your business' and individual employees' actual performance against standards (goals) you have set. If performance exceeds standards, excellent. Raise the standards a notch. If performance falls short, look for the causes, correct them and proceed.

This simple process, rigorously applied over time, improves profits, makes your business more reliable and takes very little of your time. Diagrammatically, it looks like this:

1. Decide what to measure
2. Determine standards for each measure
3. Observe and measure actual performance
4. Compare performance against standards
5. Correct or congratulate

Continue the cycle of measure/compare/correct until either you need new standards or conditions change substantially.

Some company-wide measures, especially those found on the income statement, balance sheet, and cash flow projections, should be monitored at least monthly. Individual measures such as sales prospecting calls made or number of items processed may need to be monitored weekly or daily; quality control measures may be needed even more frequently.

Does managing by the numbers work? The answer is an emphatic "yes." But managing by the numbers in a vacuum won't work. It's just another tool in your managerial toolbox which, used in conjunction with your other skills, can't do anything but help you.

The managers of major league baseball teams are exemplars of managing by the numbers. Look at what they use as measures. The won/loss record shows how they stack up as a team compared with others. The N.Y. Yankees once won five World Series championships in a row, an unequalled team performance. Team and individual statistics cover all basic baseball activities: batting, running, pitching and fielding. These can be compared to other players, to other teams, to old-time players. Ty Cobb had a .367 lifetime batting average, the all-time record, though Pete Rose got more hits during his career. Roger Maris hit 61 homers in one season, edging Babe Ruth's long-standing record of 60 home runs—though there are extenuating factors, of course, such as a longer season and more teams. Hank Aaron hit 755 home runs in his career to Babe Ruth's 729 career homers. Nolan Ryan is the all-time no hit pitching champion, with seven no-hitters to date.

These are objective standards of excellence. A .350 hitter in the big show is a star, provided he gets up to bat often enough. A 20-game winner is an automatic multimillionaire. Ted Williams' .406 batting average and Joe Dimaggio's 56 game hitting streak (both in 1941) qualify them as all time superstars.

While baseball fans are unusually interested in statistics, other sports recognize the value of heeding the numbers: Do you want to improve your golf game? Keep a record of how you play each hole next time. The time after that, check how you did before each hole. You'll improve because you have a goal (lower score) and some notion of how you did the last time. Measure and compare your performance against a standard (the basic Managing by the Numbers technique) and you gain a measure of control over your performance. There are limitations, of course. If par is 72, and you play only twice a year, the odds are against improving your usual 94. Play more often and, all things being equal, you'll improve.

This concept of limitation is important. Managing by the numbers can help your business attain its potential, but doesn't guarantee it. If you have too little capital or your markets are too small or too full of competitors, your progress will be limited, just as surely as your progress as an athlete is limited by your physical skills and will to succeed.

Back to baseball. A manager keeps track of a wide range of numbers, both team and individual, as the best way to spot weak areas (so they can be either strengthened or supported or avoided) and take advantage of strengths. The standards performances are measured against are objective: speed, wins or losses, earned run averages, runs batted in, on base average, errors. The list of standards is large but selective. Since the performance of the team is a function of individual performances, the manager wants to know who's on a hot streak, who's in a slump, who is good in the clutch, and so on. These trends are valuable information. A player who hit .240 two years ago, .280 last year, and is hitting .320 this year is more valuable than a player who goes from .320 to 280 to .240, assuming that there are no major fudge factors.

Performance over time (trends) and performance measured against objective standards are applications of Managing by the Numbers. A player in a slump may be pulled, may get extra batting practice, may get a physical to determine if there is a physiological reason or may be disciplined for staying out too late. That's up to the manager. The diagnosis is objective: "You've gone one for 35 this month" or "Your ERA has gone from 3.8 to 12.7 in six starts." Performance over time, measured against objective standards. One for 35 is lousy. So's an ERA of 12.7, at least in the major leagues. Whether the player is performing as expected isn't a question. That's one very powerful argument for incorporating Managing by the Numbers into all personnel management areas. It focuses discussion on the performance, not on the performer. It replaces personality hassles with facts.

The decision of what to measure and what standards to refer to is difficult, but in almost every sport or business or activity there are a number of guidelines to follow. Traditional measures and standards are a good place to start. In baseball (again), a big league team hopes to win 95 or more games, batters want to hit .300 or higher, pitchers want to win 20 games, fielders want a higher fielding percentage than their rivals on other teams. The absolute (.300 batting average) or comparative (higher fielding percentage) standards are equally valid. And hallowed. However: While a .300 hitter for the Boston Red Sox is rare and highly paid, .300 hitters on a Little League team are common. Some even bat .600 for a season. The context defines the standards. It makes no sense for a Little League manager to keep the kind of detailed records a fully staffed major league team finds important. That would be overkill.

The motivating power of managing by the numbers is impressive. If you believe (as I do) that people motivate themselves if you provide a way for them to mark their progress, managing by the numbers is for you. Think of the great American concern with weight. Want to lose 15 pounds? Pick a realistic, reasonable, healthful and achievable goal: lose one or two pounds a week for 10 weeks. Get a sensitive scale, follow a rational diet and weigh in at the same time every day. Chart the weight loss (gain) daily. The graphic display of the trend will keep your motivation up even in the face of occasional reversals.

If baseball players are motivated to practice harder and improve their batting by approaching .300 or golfers are motivated by the goal of finally breaking 80, think what clear goals and measurable progress towards achieving those goals will do for your employees. I assure you that their performance will improve.

Part I
Company-wide Measures

Managing by the numbers applies to both company-wide and individual performance. Although related, these measures are different. For the business, the key measures are largely derived from the three basic financial statements: the cash flow, profit and loss (also called income statement), and the balance sheet. This information is highly formatted to make comparisons between businesses or for the same business at different times much easier. Individual measures (see Part II) are more idiosyncratic and task-related.

The basic financial statements are not the only numbers source for managing by the numbers, although they are the most familiar and important. Individual business owners have devised numerous shortcuts including key factors or measures for their own business, and summary forms to help them control the unruly tides of information which threaten to drown their patience. Information overload is a problem: How and where should you stem the flow?

Interviews with small business owners, experts, bankers and others yield these rules of thumb:

1. Keep track of the trends of your sales revenue, gross margin, operating expenses, available capital (credit line), profit/loss on a monthly basis. Or more frequently.

2. Cash flow = survival.

3. Businesses without budgets go broke.

4. You can never have too much capital, but probably don't have enough.

5. Sales and marketing take precedence over finance.

The problems managing by the numbers reveals are ultimately marketing problems. All expenses are tied to marketing decisions. Revenues rise or fall with marketing efforts; capital is raised, depleted or denied in light of how marketing is (or promises to be) effective.

For managing by the numbers to be effective in your business, you must have adequate bookkeeping and accounting. I have made the assumption that you already have a good information system, an accountant who can help you understand how your system works, and are getting timely information. Monthly P & Ls and balance sheets, thanks to computers, are available for the smallest company. While a "one-write" system can provide monthly statements for confirmed computerphobes, the cost of a powerful microcomputer is so low, and the availability of good user-friendly accounting and bookkeeping software so high, that it takes a willful business owner to forgo the benefits of a computer.

Chapter 1
Limiting Information

Key Factors

You start managing by the numbers by deciding what to measure. Beyond the obvious (see below) this becomes problematic. Every business has some make-or-break factors, critically important to its success, that go beyond the financial statements. They are relevant to the financials, but don't show up as normal items.

• Motels are dependent on their occupancy rate. If an occupancy rate of 70% is necessary to break even, the astute operator keeps a weather eye on the strength of the economy, price structures, competitive moves and advertising. A slow economy will often manifest itself in reduced business and vacation travel, which shows up in the occupancy rate.

• Manufacturers follow the balance of bookings, billings and backlog. A smooth balance keeps production profitable, whereas an imbalance (no new business booked, billings down, backlog falling off) betokens trouble. Quality complaints and returns are other focus points, easily tracked.

• Grocers worry about stockouts and spoilage. Restaurant owners count covers and watch for pilferage and delivery problems. Publishers keep a close eye on inventory and returns. They also need to keep a steady stream of new editorial ideas.

How do you learn what factors to keep an eye on? Look at the big items first. Fine tune later. What you look for first are indicators that profits, cash flow and market share are all trending in the right direction. By focusing on the big picture you set the groundwork for concentrating efforts where they pay off best.

• Is your business profitable? If not, why not? If it is, is the trend up, down or flat?

• Is cash flow positive? You need both positive cash flow and consistent operating profits to survive and grow.

• Are most of your expenses variable? Then control costs. If the majority of your expenses are fixed, you make money by driving the top line.

• How big are your target markets?

• What is your penetration and potential in those markets?

Next, look for "drop dead" factors. These are the items that could put you out of business if they get out of control.

• What is your cash and liquidity situation? Liquidity is the ability to meet short term debt, in particular tax, trade and bank obligations. The "burn rate," the speed with which continued negative cash flow will put you out of business, is the prototypical drop-dead factor.

• What would shut you down? If you live by the phone, make sure your phones don't get shut off. If you make ice cream, make sure your electric bill is paid so your freezers keep running.

You have to determine what your business' leverage points are. How can you economically locate the key factors? Read and listen. Start by reading publications put out by your trade association. Key, critical or leverage factors are common editorial subjects. Look through back issues. Call the editors or trade association executives, or communicate directly with authors who have piqued your interest. Go to trade shows and talk with other business owners. Many trade shows have seminars, and the persons who lead the seminars are a rich source of ideas, expertise and techniques. Ask for their phone numbers and tell them you'll call if you need advice. They'll be flattered.

Above all, do not try to reinvent the wheel. It's silly to squander time uncovering steps others have long since discovered. Once you have a firm grasp of the basic leverage points, then you can try to explore new territory.

• Ask your key employees for their ideas. What do they think are important leverage points? How do they keep on top of their jobs?

• Ask outsiders for help. Consultants, educators, accountants, vendors, Small Business Administration personnel (SCORE and SBDC counselors for general information, SBI programs for specific problems) are an excellent low or no-cost resource. Competitors, especially from afar, are sometimes willing to share ideas with you. Canon encourages round-table discussions which generate a lot of specific camera dealer information. Certain colleges have specialties and can provide highly customized advice. For instance, Cornell University's School of Hotel Administration is staffed by leading hospitality industry experts.

If this looks like a big task, rest easy. While there are some methods to make sure budgets and projections are being followed, the information can be entered by your bookkeeper. Your job is to interpret the information and formulate strategies to improve your business operations and profitability, based on facts rather than impressions or hunches.

The Blackford Files

John Blackford, a financial consultant based in Concord, N.H., says it is important to keep information simple, preferably on one page. His client files contain forms that display line items from the P & L (simplified to avoid information overload), historical or trade data to see how the business is trending and five key items from the balance sheet. This is more than enough information to monitor business operations. If any numbers are out of line, the warning flags go up: What's the cause? Is this good or bad?

Managing by the numbers directs attention to variances from anticipated norms. The trend of variances across months as well as the absolute and relative size of the individual monthly variances from the norm are important. You have to use your judgment to decide when to press the alarm buzzer and take action. The variance report implicit in Mr. Blackford's method is a powerful tool.

Keep the information on a single page. This makes its use more probable. Nothing is more daunting to an action-oriented entrepreneur than a thick wad of undigested data. Hence Mr. Blackford's emphasis on putting the information needed to flag coming problems on one sheet. The comparisons are easily made, variances spotted, and attention directed to the appropriate areas.

There are two ways to record the numbers on your financial statements: absolute numbers, which are the dollar figures, or percentages of total sales (for the profit and loss statement) or percentage of total assets (for the balance sheet). Sometimes a dollar change is less revealing than a percentage change; sometimes it goes the other way. "Common sizing," measuring line items as percent of sales (or percent of assets), simplifies comparisons. It's easy to do:

$$(\text{P\&L line item} \div \text{gross sales}) \times 100 = \text{common-sized P \& L}$$

$$(\text{Balance sheet line item} \div \text{total assets}) \times 100 = \text{common-sized balance sheet}$$

Total assets

The five conventional financial measures mentioned earlier (net sales, gross margin, operating expense, available capital and profit or loss) take almost no time to review. You'll have to decide what constitutes a significant fluctuation. In the normal course of events your business has seasonal flows. A change in sales may be important or may just reflect seasonality. A change in numbers, given the context of your business, will cause you to react differently once you understand the cause.

• **Sales revenues** drive most businesses. You don't have a business if you don't generate sufficient sales revenue. Any major changes demand immediate and careful attention.

Keep in mind that

$$\text{Sales revenue} = \text{units times price}$$

The units may be things, hours or services provided. Total revenue can always be broken down this way, and if there has been a change in revenue patterns, this is the first place to look for problems. Either your unit sales are off, or prices are off, or both.

• **Gross margin** (sales less cost of goods sold) is the single most important measure from your P&L. Most operating expenses are relatively stable and must be covered by the gross margin. Declines in the gross margin may reflect lowered sales activity, pricing problems or cost-of-goods-sold difficulties.

"Guard thy margins" is always good advice. One problem business owners create for themselves is increasing sales levels by cutting prices. The impact on the gross margin can be disastrous.

$$\Delta \text{ Gross margin} = \Delta \text{ unit sales}, \Delta \text{ price}, \Delta \text{ COGS}$$

(Δ denotes change. Thus "Δ Sales" means "change in sales.") If you detect a change in gross margin, either as an absolute dollar figure or as a percentage of revenues, look to the right side of the equation for a first approximation of where the problem might be rooted. The red flag that pops up helps you focus your attention on certain areas. You may have to dig deeper to find the cause of the change. For example, sales levels and prices may be fine, but COGS is up. Now you'd look into the components of cost of goods sold. You'll seldom find a simple cause. More likely you'll find a series of inter-connected factors that, in concert, cause the change you observe.

• **Operating expenses** tend to be fixed, that is they don't change with sales level. Their total tends to be stable, so if there is a change, look to the individual line items.

The most common reason for a fluctuation in operating expenses is the five-paycheck month (three-paycheck if you pay biweekly). Look for this first. Your sales and gross margin are fine but operating expense is up. How come? If you have added employees, or given raises, operating expenses will change.

If the change is not due to these obvious factors, then following the rule of look for the large numbers first go through the individual line items. The explanation may be as simple as an unexpectedly high utility bill or failure to pay the rent.

Δ Operating Expenses: first look for Δ in numbers of pay periods or Δ in number of employees or Δ in salaries. Then look to: Δ in line items (look for timing problems here too).

• **Available capital.** Small businesses stand or fall on their ability to generate cash. Having enough working capital (current assets minus current liabilities) is one way to measure this, but all too often working capital looks swell but is largely tied up in ac-counts receivable, inventories, or both. This is another example of a "drop-dead" mea-sure. Run out of cash (including available credit) and you're out of business.

You track available capital to make sure you don't get caught in a liquidity squeeze. Trade credit is not a source of available capital. The worst financial advice given small business owners is "lean on trade" or "stretch payables." While this may work as a very short term expedient, your trade creditors wise up and will be swift to shut you down.

Cash is the lifeblood of the firm. The cash-flow budget (see Ch 7) provides a way to predict and control your cash and liquidity needs.

• **Profit (loss)** is the bottom line. Subtract operating expenses from your gross margin and get your monthly report card.

You can improve profits by increasing gross margin, cutting expenses or both. Deciding which, how and when is the duty and pleasure of management. If profits are up you want to know why. It may be because sales are strong, margins are holding and costs are under control.

On the other hand you may have booked sales before they occurred, forgotten a major expense, or missed a tax payment. There are dangerous ways to make a profit: For ex-ample, sell off inventories and don't replace them.

The bottom line on the bottom line is that yes, it is an important first-level measure of how well your business is doing but it is at most an aggregate figure and much more re-vealing in its disaggregation. Profitability is the result of doing many things right. Profit or loss is only informative in context as an indicator of managerial performance and compared with trade and historical figures.

The comparisons should be both absolute (how many dollars?) and common-size (profit as percentage of sales). For most businesses, the best measure of profitability is profit or loss pre-tax, which keeps tax complications out of the picture. Let your accountant find ways to minimize your tax burden. Focus your efforts on maintaining profitability and positive cash flow.

Points to keep in mind

• The numbers from the financial statements are only informative when examined in context. These contexts include your experience in and knowledge of your business and industry, which provide the first-level standards against which to measure the numbers.

• Detailed comparisons are helpful. These include trade or industry figures as well as historical and projected figures for your business.

• The trends of the numbers matter. So does seasonality, which can obscure trends.

• A minimum comparison period for monthly statements is three months, which tends to even out small aberrations on the monthly statements. Many business owners also use last year's average monthlies, year-to-date to compare January of this year to January of last, and "rolling quarters" in which the current month and two previous are used to compare to similar periods (either last year or a month ago). These techniques smooth out temporary aberrations, yet allow you to pick up fast on anything unusual.

• Managing by the numbers proceeds from the gross aggregate figures down to individual line items and from the line items to their composite activities. You only go as far as you need to to locate and take advantage of or correct the reasons for the aberration. The ability to do this reflexively and automatically comes only with long experience. Anomaly recognition is a useful management skill that can be developed and made fruitful by Managing by the numbers. Few of us are gifted enough to know the standards and goals to mark differences from norms and standards without recourse to written information.

• As you move from noticing anomalies to identifying their causes, remain aware of the interplay between the various parts of your business. A sales slump may alert you to a personnel problem (a salesperson taking early though unannounced semi-retirement), a competitive problem (a new and hungry competitor has entered the market), quality problems (making the sales effort harder), economic shifts (a cutback in defense spells trouble for more than defense industry suppliers) and under-capitalization, a competitive handicap similar to wearing lead shoes when playing basketball. Under-capitalization slows you up and weighs you down. A single "cause" is rare. The large problems make their presence clear; subtle problems hide and disguise themselves. The problem you note (sales down) is the tip of the iceberg. Your task is understanding that iceberg: its size, age, momentum, danger to you and so on.

• The question of salaries ("Am I paying too much? What do others pay?") is easy to address. Every state's Department of Labor keeps close watch on local and regional salaries and wages and publishes this information monthly. Your Chamber of Commerce will have this on hand. Ask other local employers. They have the same questions about what to pay their employees as you do. Check want ads to see what other companies, especially larger ones, are offering for positions similar to those in your business. Temporary help and employment agencies can also provide salary information.

• Finally—the measures discussed so far look backward. They are inherently defensive ("What went wrong?") rather than positive and goal-directed. Managing by the numbers helps you keep your business and employees focused on the goals you set. The backward looks are necessary but not the most rewarding aspect of managing by the numbers.

Chapter 2
Forecasts, Goals and Standards

Managing by the numbers works by comparing actual performance to standards. The standards must be objective, measurable, and realistic. In baseball, you want your batters to reach or exceed .300, but don't plan on them batting .400 or better. Trying to attain the unreachable is fine for saints but downright demoralizing to the rest of us.

Goals are easy to set, standards simple to choose. But to do it well is another matter. For a goal or standard to be believable, your employees (and you) have to feel that you have the resources and strategies to make that goal happen and have benchmarks along the way to keep your attention and enthusiasm up. If you think the goal is achievable, and it is not, no matter what you do or how hard you strive, the next set of goals will be less readily accepted.

Standards include goals, objectives, averages (especially trade or industrial data), forecasts and restatements of past performance. Put another way, goals and objectives are a special kind of standard. Averages function as a standard to measure performance against, though except in dire straits you wouldn't set them up as goals. "Be average!" is a poor rallying cry. Forecasts are based on your minimum goals or objectives, and become your budgets (a special form of goal) which establish the minimum acceptable level of performance. Historical performance is a fine indicator of historical performance. "Yes, that's what we did last year…" but unless you are inert or in a defensive mode, last year is merely a foundation for this year's goals. Last year's performance is normally used as the basis for a worst-case scenario, but in times of economic stress could be a difficult goal to achieve.

The goals you set for your business' near future, based on the resources and markets available, find their expression in your forecasts. You have to ground your forecasts on a firmer foundation than wishful thinking (see below), but if you think small you'll react small. Check your goals against both historical performance and industry/trade figures. These sets of figures provide a reality check. Your numbers shouldn't be copies of either, but adaptations of both. Significant differences should be closely looked at and understood, if only to forestall second-guessing by your banker.

Forecasts, especially sales forecasts, have a slippery quality even when you have carefully examined your business, its customers and competition, economic climate and all the other factors that affect your chances of reaching those goals and making your forecasts come true. This slipperiness is the main reason to dwell at length on how to create a worthwhile sales forecast. It is hard work. There are no valid shortcuts.

Forecasting and goal-setting go on concurrently. The sequence is roughly this:

1. Set goals
2. Express the goals in dollars or other numbers:
    Profit-and-loss forecast (three-year)
    Cash-flow forecast (three-year)
3. Project the balance sheet one year out to reflect profit and loss and cash-flow changes
4. Compare profit and loss and balance sheet forecasts to:
    a) historical performance
    b) trade figures
5. Revise goals and forecasts, if needed

The criteria implicit throughout this process are loose: "makes good sense for my business," "realistic goals for my business under given conditions," and "these goals are worth committing ourselves to achieving." Your understanding and experience, aided by research, afford the best reality check on the goals and forecasts, and that grounding in reality is a key element in preparing useful goals and forecasts.

Goal setting

The goals you set for your business are as much a function of the age and stage of your business as they are of your ambitions. Approaching goal setting systematically helps keep the goals realistic and differentiates goal setting from wishful thinking.

Even before setting down the initial numbers in your sales and expense forecasts, review your goals. These come in two flavors: your personal goals, which are primary, and your goals for your business over the next few years. Your business goals are subordinate to your personal goals, or should be, even though the two sets are most likely intertwined. Your business life should support your personal life. That is, if you want to retire in five years to travel, or sell your business in two years to pursue another activity, your goals for the business would be different than if you plan to grow the business indefinitely because it's so much fun to do so. The broad, often subjective personal goals provide subtle limits on business plans, which have to be very specific.

Companies in a start-up or other transition phase pose a particular problem: they will almost always veer from their initial goals. "Transitional" companies come in several guises. Unlike the start-up business, a transitional business has a history to help guide it and define goals. But during the transitional period (shift of ownership or management, major changes in the marketplace or technology or economy), it is much more like a start-up than an ongoing business. Goals tend to be very fluid; similar businesses are hard to locate because most trade and industry data are based on the average performance; and historical performance is no longer pertinent. Because the business must in some critical sense be reestablished, with completely or substantively new goals and forecasts, treat a company in transition as if it were a start-up. This is especially important in a turnaround where the company has lost all momentum and must be started up anew.

Fast-growth companies are driven by their markets, which makes goal setting beyond "meet the demand" and "don't run out of cash" extremely difficult. The most important goal is liquidity. Fast growth devours cash at a frightening pace. This does not mean that you needn't set goals and make forecasts if you are riding a fast-growth business. You should—but be prepared to shift gears and rethink both goals and forecasts much more frequently than in the other genres. Start-up, transitional and ongoing businesses will normally function well with goals and plans revised no more often than every six months (or a year, if the forecasts hold up). Fast-growth businesses need to rethink their numbers as often as monthly and at all times have a contingency plan available to meet the threat of running out of cash.

In the business planning process you start with your notions of what business you are really in, move to a careful consideration of what you sell and then turn to a close scrutiny of your targeted markets. This is easier for an ongoing business than a start-up/transition or fast-growth business but the same principles apply to them as well.

Key questions

• What business are you really in? Or: What is your "mission statement" or reason to be in business? This is a short statement that defines your business. As an example, the mission statement of the publisher of this book is "to provide useful, applicable management tools or publications to owners, managers and advisors of small businesses." This is narrow enough to keep them focused, broad enough to permit some latitude.

• What do you sell? What do your customers think you sell? You may find that you don't know what you're selling, if what you sell is defined as what your customers buy. "My factories manufacture cosmetics," Charles Revson said. "We sell hope." He knew what he was selling.

• Who are your target markets? The individuals who constitute your core market should be very familiar to you. Not necessarily by name (unless your markets are extremely small), but rather by demographic descriptions (age, income, gender, educational level, lifestyles and so forth). Even if you sell to industrial or institutional markets you sell to specific individuals. Who are they? What are they like? What are their titles? Who is involved in making the purchasing decision (influencers as well as gatekeepers)? Why, how and when do they buy? This is vitally important knowledge. If you don't have it, drop everything and set about getting it. Now.

• How large are your markets?

• What is (will be) your share of those markets? Questions of market size and market share are slippery. A market that is defined too tightly will be too small to permit growth or even survival. One hundred percent of a market of one is one customer. Markets designed too loosely ("Everybody is a prospect! Five billion people need this product!") cannot be reached by any business, small or Fortune 100. The key is to be realistic. Retail trade associations keep track of how many people are needed to support a store. If the trade experts say 20,000 people (population of market area) are needed, and you are in a city of 40,000 with only one competitor, fine. Seek out and use these numbers.

Fortunately for all of us small business owners, market size, market share and demographics are heavily studied. Research librarians can help you locate, understand and use information ranging from the most recent census to more arcane demographic studies. Small Business Institutes (an SBA program) and almost every business school can help you apply this kind of information to your own business. You want to make sure that your market is large enough to be profitable, small enough to be defended against competitors, and growing enough to satisfy your growth plans.

This is not simple but it is an important part of managing by the numbers. Market share studies help you create realistic sales forecasts and budgets.

• Who are your competitors? What share of the market do they enjoy? What is their pricing strategy? While price competition is usually the worst financial strategy, it's very common. Keep an eye on the competition and you can benefit from imitating their successes and avoiding their errors. Just keeping files on your five nearest competitors will put you in the competitive driver's seat. Use a manila folder, one per competitor, for clippings and notes. Any information is helpful, but ads from newspapers, legal filings, brochures and price sheets form the core.

• What resources can you allocate to projected sales growth? Growth devours excess cash, capital and credit, then gnaws at your basic running needs. The cash flow forecast helps define the limits of growth. So does the "Index of Sustainable Financial Growth" found in Chapter 10, 'Strategic Analysis." While energetic growth goals are fine to pursue, prudence demands that you be able to fund that growth. Otherwise you'll fall short or go broke.

• What personnel and management do you (will you) have available to implement your plans?

There are many other factors to ponder in a business plan, but these eight questions are a good beginning. Your answers to them will help you set the goals embodied in your actual forecast.

Before proceeding to the forecasts, speak with your sales and marketing staff (sales manager, marketing manager, sales reps) for advice on what sales levels are reasonable. In a very small business, everyone will have ideas to offer. In *Forecasting Sales and Planning Profits* (see Bibliography), Kenneth Marino poses a strong argument in favor of what he calls an "MP–SR" (Market Potential–Sales Requirement) system. He suggests that you use marketing research to set sales goals (top down) and sales requirements to cover costs and profits (bottom up). Your sales force will help you determine whether or not the "SR" goals are reasonable.

Sales forecasting

Establishing a sales forecast is the first step in putting your goals into numbers. Sales drive every business, whether brand new, in transition or just chugging along. They affect all expenses, if only in a negative way (if you have no sales, how do you pay the bills?).

Some expenses are fixed within the limits of a certain sales range, while others vary directly with sales, which is another reason to start with sales forecasting.

The forecasting process

Set goals
⬇
Forecast sales
⬇
Prepare expense forecast
⬇
Prepare profit-and-loss projections
⬇
Prepare cash-flow pro forma
⬇
Forecast capital needs

All forecasts are based on assumptions and hunches, a meld of information and experience. They won't be 100% accurate. That's fine. One hundred percent accuracy is unattainable and in many cases an excuse for inaction. A 95% accuracy level would be outstanding. You'd do well to hit 90%—and even then occasionally be surprised.

Start with your sales goals. What is the composition of those sales and the likelihood of attaining them? Both the P&L and cash-flow projections start with sales. The method I suggest is highly effective for short-term (up to one year) forecasts. Two or three year goals are less accurate, but provide some direction for your business, and as you will revise your forecasts at least annually, tend to self-correct. If you need to forecast beyond three years you'll be in the realm of pure guesswork. Even forecasting beyond six months or one year is fraught with pitfalls. The distant numbers you generate have a specious aura of authority ("Let's see: five years' compounded annual growth rate of 30 per cent...") that reality laughs at. This is one place where computerized spreadsheets can lead anyone astray.

As you follow the sales forecasting process, make notes. The assumptions you base your numbers on are derived from your experience and should be checked against industry and historical figures as part of the full forecasting process. If you forget to document your assumptions as you go along, it's unlikely that you'll remember what those assumptions were several weeks or months later. Scrutinizing your assumptions (in order to correct and improve them) is an integral part of managing by the numbers that is easily overlooked.

Method 1

Some owners and managers like to forecast sales by starting with profit goals, following the dictum "profit is a fixed expense." If your business traditionally achieves 15% pre-tax profit on sales, then a simple calculation determines the sales levels you need to attain a projected dollar profit:

$$Profit\ (pre\text{-}tax)\ as\ per\ cent\ of\ sales = 15\%$$

$$Projected\ profit\ (goal) = \$60,000$$

$$Sales\ needed = \$60,000 \div 0.15 = \$400,000$$

This method is not recommended for either start-up/transitional or fast-growth businesses. If you don't have a consistent profitability picture (these kinds of businesses don't by definition), any profitability percentage is as good as any other. For an ongoing business, it can be a very helpful check on the sales figures derived by Method 2 below—this is how I use it.

Method 2

In order to avoid wrestling with a lump sales figure, break the gross figure into its component parts. Product lines are one way to do this. Another useful method is to divide sales by market area: so much to industrial, so much to institutional, so much to individual. Or by sales method: direct sales, retail sales. Each of us has a pet methods of creating sales forecasts. Mine is: Build up sales forecasts by product line and market segments. This generates useful numbers.

Determine, for each product line or market segment, the most likely annual sales by figuring the "worst case," the "best case," and then the "most likely case." The resulting total sales figure is a construct that you can use with fair confidence. It is not a grab at thin air. Examples are provided below to indicate several ways to dice your onions. It begins with a look at last year's sales, broken down by market segment. (It could have been broken down by product line; this is a matter of choice.)

Last year's sales

Independent stores	$45,000
Chain stores	125,000
Individual (direct)	24,000
Government	85,000
Banks	33,000
Foreign	32,000
Other	12,000
TOTAL	356,000

Sales forecast form

	Worst case	Most likely	Best case
A. Independent stores	_____	_____	_____
B. Chain stores	_____	_____	_____
C. Individual (direct)	_____	_____	_____
D. Government	_____	_____	_____
E. Banks	_____	_____	_____
F. Foreign	_____	_____	_____
G. Other	_____	_____	_____
TOTAL	_____	_____	_____

The procedure is this: For each product or market segment (A, B, C, ...) list the "worst-case" sales. This is what you can see happening if everything goes wrong. The economy sours, your customers find other suppliers, new competitors enter the fray, price wars break out, your sales force defects. Everything goes wrong that can go wrong. This highly unlikely scenario is useful for a couple of reasons. First, it will later be the basis for your contingency plan, which is handy in case your banker desires to see it. Second, by looking at what might go wrong on an incremental basis, you can't help but look ahead—and thus avoid pitfalls.

This is the essence of managing by the numbers. The process of putting the numbers together forces you to look at your business differently.

Look at the example below. Suppose you sell a line of products to these seven markets. "Other" includes atypical sources of revenue such as consulting or installation fees.

Worst-case sales (by target market)

	Worst case	Most likely	Best case
Independent stores	$40,000	_____	_____
Chain stores	120,000	_____	_____
Individual (direct)	20,000	_____	_____
Government	80,000	_____	_____
Banks	30,000	_____	_____
Foreign	30,000	_____	_____
Other	10,000	_____	_____
TOTAL	330,000	_____	_____

Ordinarily, if these markets are or "feel" stable, and if you have no intimation of radical change, and if you don't plan any unusual activities, you can expect to come close to last year's sales figures as a "worst-case" scenario. "Close" means in the 90% range. If you sold $45,000 to a particular market segment last year, this year you'd be distressed and surprised to do worse than $40,000 (89% of last year's sales).

The process continues. Use historical figures, tempered by your experience and the judgment of your sales force, and look at each major market in turn. The net result: worst-case sales total $330,000.

Now for the fun part. What do you think your best case would be? The same kind of analysis goes on. New products are well received, old products continue to chip in sales, new opportunities come up. This is not a pie-in-the-sky exercise, but a carefully thought out "what if" scenario. You don't expect a new item to sell 100,000 units in its first year. You'd like it, but the chances are so remote you shouldn't let it infect the forecasting process. Nor do you assume that there is a pent-up demand for your products in declining markets. Each best-case figure represents a mini scenario.

The forecasts reflect reasoned judgements, estimates based on your knowledge of and experience with your products and markets. Not on trade averages, not on wishful thinking, not on fantasy or magic. If your forecasts are to be useful, they must represent the quantification of your conclusions drawn from your experience, research, hunches and goals. You need research (including input from employees and other people) and facts (such as trade data) to test your forecasts. But your forecasts ultimately embody *your* ideas. That's one satisfaction of being the boss.

Keep notes to remind you how you arrived at our figures. A simplified version is as follows.

Best case sales by market

	Worst case	*Most likely*	*Best case*
Independent stores	$40,000	_____	$90,000
Chain stores	120,000	_____	190,000
Individual (direct)	20,000	_____	40,000
Government	80,000	_____	110,000
Banks	30,000	_____	30,000
Foreign	30,000	_____	50,000
Other	10,000	_____	20,000
TOTAL	$330,000	_____	$530,000

Notes: Independent store sales can be doubled with more aggressive marketing and a few new products. Sales of old products should increase by at least $10,000. After this year, slower growth is anticipated. (Sales forecast up $45,000 over last year.)

Chain-store sales are growing with increased sales efforts. Reorders of old products are also higher and can be increased with a more focused effort. (Sales forecast up $65,000 over last year.)

Sales to individuals (direct sales) should be a growth market. Last year's sales were down because of a lack of marketing effort. (Sales forecast up $16,000 over last year.)

Government markets continue to strengthen. (Sales forecast up $25,000 over last year.)

Bank sales slumped last year; no change foreseen this year or next, no matter what we do. But we will maintain a presence in this market. (Sales forecast down $3,000 from last year.)

Foreign sales are up sharply, especially in Eastern Europe and Australia. New sales agents and attendance at international trade shows should lead to significant sales increases. (Sales forecast up $18,000 over last year.)

Other: fluctuates; expect increase from new product lines. (Sales forecast to be up $8,000 over last year.)

Please notice that in this part of the forecasting process you are examining strategies to help reach the goals implicit in the "best case" scenarios. Always plan for growth unless you have strong reasons not to.

In the "worst-case" scenario, look at problems you might face. What are the pitfalls and barriers? In the "best case" you are more interested in positive opportunities and ways to increase sales. In the final step, the "most likely" scenario, pull these ideas together to better understand your opportunities and form strategies to take advantage of them. The "most likely" scenario shapes the structure and content of the operating budgets, the P&L and cash-flow pro formas that become key company-wide standards. It also provides a third run-through of your forecast.

Three separate forecasts may look like overkill, but it is not an onerous chore. The benefits are huge: each run-through gives you another structured chance to test your assumptions and examine tactics and strategies. Managing by the numbers' greatest benefits come from this kind of focused attention.

Most likely sales by market

Last year		Worst case	Most likely	Best case	Increase
$45,000	Independent stores	$40,000	$80,000	$90,000	+100%
125,000	Chain stores	120,000	175,000	190,000	+52%
24,000	Individual (direct)	20,000	30,000	40,000	+66%
85,000	Government	80,000	90,000	110,000	+30%
33,000	Banks	30,000	30,000	30,000	-10%
32,000	Foreign	30,000	45,000	50,000	+56%
12,000	Other	10,000	15,000	20,000	+66%
$356,000		$330,000	$465,000	$530,000	+49%

The largest potential increases deserve the most attention. Managing by the numbers tries to get you the best return on your efforts, and this will come from focusing efforts on the markets with best potential. This does not mean that you should neglect any of your business. It means you should set priorities.

Since you have good reasons to expect significant increases in independent, chain-store and foreign markets, the "most likely" figures are skewed towards "best case." Mild increases are expected elsewhere (remember: your "worst case" scenario assumes sales no worse than 90% of last year's), with the exception of the bank market, which you expect to remain dormant.

Each line is a scenario. The "most likely" case for each market is based on your knowledge of your products and markets, continuously updated. Don't take a simple average of "worst case" and "best case." To do so cripples the forecasting process.

Depending on what kind of business you are in, you would choose different ways to split up your markets, products, or services.

If you run a country inn you might look at food, liquor, rooms, other.

If you distribute ball bearings, you might consider breaking the markets by salesperson and sales territory.

If you are a lawyer, you could project by professional fees, research, clerical/support.

A gift-shop owner might examine the prospects for books, magazines, cards, gifts, sundries.

The point is simple: Don't try to forecast the total sales, then break it into components. Start with the components and build upwards to the total.

Some questions to ask about each profit center or product line are:
• What is the potential for one year? For five years out?
• How easily can we make this grow?
• What are the margins?
• How much will it cost (dollars, people) to achieve this growth? Can we afford it?
• Are the trends up or down?

Don't try to break out more than eight or ten product lines, markets, divisions or other components. If you do, you'll lose sight of the forest in a welter of trees. For most businesses, four or five are sufficient.

Special case 1: start-ups

Start-ups have particularly difficult sales-forecasting problems. Difficult but not insoluble. With no prior sales experience for the business, other guidelines are needed.

The danger is ignoring the first law of business physics: a business at rest tends to remain at rest. Trade and industry figures are derived from the performance of ongoing businesses. This skews the figures. New businesses tend to have sales lower than their expenses might justify, and all too often less capital than they really need to get sales up to a profitable level.

What's the solution? The same three-column forecasting approach will work. To be conservative, figure the "best case" first, basing it on the top performers' performance (see the top quartile of Robert Morris Associates' or Financial Research Associates' trade figures). At best you'll be able to get to this level in the first year. You presumably think you can; otherwise, why go into business? But it is unlikely that you'll do better.

1. Look at the ratio of sales to net worth. This enables you to estimate the level of sales you could attain given the capital invested in the business. The amount of capital invested or borrowed helps determine the sales level you can reach. This becomes crucial for growing businesses, as their receivables tend to outstrip their capital base. Beyond a certain point, lenders won't provide capital for fast growth and will require more invested capital. This leverage problem is a particularly irksome thorn in the flesh of rapidly growing businesses.

While net worth and invested capital aren't always the same, they are at start-up, since there are no retained earnings. If the top quartile has a sales to net worth ratio of 15 and you have $50,000 invested capital, sales in the $750,000 range, while improbable, are possible. The worst case and most likely case are then roughed in (as before, your judgment and experience play their role here), and you end up with an aggregate sales figure. Break this out as a reality check.

2. Once you have established the "most likely" range, take the figures to your banker, financial advisor or other trusted expert. Be prepared to have your figures challenged. It pays off. Remember: the payoff is in the performance, not in the projections.

3. Redo your forecasts. Time spent here pays you back in numerous areas. You will develop more realistic sales forecasts, you will go through a minimum of six iterations and will develop greater understanding of your proposed business.

Your forecasts become the working model of your business, once you add the expenses and debt loads. The P&L and cash flow are designed to provide a working model of your business. A reasonableness criterion is implicit: are these numbers reasonable, given the economic and competitive situation you find yourself in?

Special case 2: transitional businesses

Turnarounds and ownership changes result in a slightly different set of problems. There is an operating history to serve as a worst-case guide, but there is some question of how applicable that history is. If the business is in a slide, a negative momentum develops. You have to first halt the slide, then reverse the momentum; this is always harder and takes longer than you expect. Most ownership changes involve some loss of momentum, if only because a few employees are going to be distracted or a few key customers might defect.

All transitional businesses need a completely new business plan. A key part of this plan is a fresh look at both products/services and markets. Unlike an ongoing business which has a wide range of ways to forecast sales, transitional businesses must reexamine both sides of the product/market mix.

Do two sales forecasts. One sales forecast should be by product lines, a second by major market segments. This forces attention to your customers. The same "worst case/best case" process is used as before.

Transitional business forecasting

Year before last	Last year	Current year (annualized)	Worst case
$300,000 $240,000 if annualized	$270,000	$180,000 for 9 months	$144,000

Here's an example of a serious decline. The current year's performance is annualized by extrapolating from nine months' performance. If the actual figures are

$80,000	first quarter
$60,000	second quarter
$40,000	third quarter

the annualization would be considerably lower. If the fourth quarter is the strongest in most years, the annualization might be higher. Look at how the numbers are generated before jumping to conclusions. While the example uses 90% of the previous year's sales, excepting unusual cases, use a lower multiplier. How low depends on the severity of the transition. A turnaround might look at a 40% or 50% factor; an ownership change, well-orchestrated and smooth, 80% to 90%. The percentages will vary. There is no mechanical way to grind them out. Too much judgment is involved.

Historic momentum is more powerful than trade averages in figuring the near-term forecast, especially when tempered by your knowledge of current economic and market conditions. Once again, test your forecasts against those of your banker, financial advisor or other expert. Since you are new to this business, or are trying to effect a dramatic change in direction of one you know well, get all the help you can. Your banker will very likely haul out the trade data. This is helpful, if somewhat beside the point, but it forces yet another look at your assumptions and is valuable if only for that reason.

Special case 3: fast growth

If you are the owner of a fast-growth business, you need two separate forecasts, one assuming the fast growth will continue, the other assuming that it will not.

Fast-growth sales forecast

	Slow growth			Fast growth		
	Worst	*Most likely*	*Best*	*Worst*	*Most likely*	*Best*
A.	_____	_____	_____	_____	_____	_____
B.	_____	_____	_____	_____	_____	_____
C.	_____	_____	_____	_____	_____	_____
D.	_____	_____	_____	_____	_____	_____
E.	_____	_____	_____	_____	_____	_____
TOTALS	_____	_____	_____	_____	_____	_____

You need both of these forecasts to satisfy your creditors, vendors, bankers and your own information needs. The first helps you get a handle on your cash and capital needs. The second provides a fallback plan, a lowered set of cash and capital needs. Fast growth doesn't last forever, and if you continue to grow, you'll be hiring experts to help with a much different level of managing by the numbers, one well beyond the scope of this book.

You also will have to revise your sales forecast more frequently than either start-up/transitional or ongoing businesses. Where they would revise no more often than every six months, if not just once a year, fast growth demands continual revisions to the sales forecast. It is extremely important to detect changes in sales and cash flow patterns quickly. If you don't demand this of yourself, your bankers will, because fast growth equals high risk. New entries in exploding markets can be abruptly swamped by large companies. Look at IBM's devastating impact on the microcomputer industry in the

1980s. They waited until the market began to boom, *then* jumped in and seized a lion's share of the market.

Neither history nor trade figures are much help in the continued fast-growth scenario. You may be able to find analogous businesses, which while not in precisely the same industry, are close by reason of product, market or structure. There may be no trade data worth using; fast-growth businesses tend to be found in fast-growth sectors of the economy. Even in retailing, a new concept (e.g., discounted toys) can be used to carve a new industry niché. Not until after the fast-growth years are over will you find really helpful trade data.

Forecasting sales and planning profits

Your sales forecast is almost finished, but not quite. Two important operations have to be performed on it: First you have to extrapolate or extend it to three years (five if your financial sources insist). Second, you have to take the annual figures and break them down by month. I recommend monthly for the first year, quarterly for years two through five.

Long-range sales forecasting in a small business is a chancy affair. You can extrapolate current trends: if you have enjoyed 15% annual sales growth and anticipate continued growth, extrapolation works. You can use linear regression analysis on changes in annual growth rates (a method used in fisCAL ™), consult chicken entrails, or even consult an economist. You still are going to be extrapolating guesses guided by your experience.

Why forecast two to five years out, then? It helps to lay out goals, to see what your business would look like if the sales forecasts are met. The value is in the forecasting process itself, the questions you raise and answer. They help you arrange financing—bankers love forecasts. They guide you in the paths of fiscal prudence. They help you spot opportunities before your competitors do. Just thinking in long time frames provides a measure of directional stability: we want these sales levels in three years; what do we have to do between now and then to reach that goal?

Since you should prepare sales forecasts at least once a year, preferably more often, any egregious errors will be corrected over time. If your long-term plans call for expansion, these forecasts help you understand your business's capital needs (your cash-flow projection will give you a good estimate of the necessary amount and its timing) as well as the kind of financing most apt to be secured.

As for any direct operational value of these long-range forecasts (beyond helping you investigate various scenarios), there is little. The one-year budgets provide the operational control. The long-range budgets establish a framework for planning.

Long-range questions to ask yourself

• What are your plans? For example, if you open other stores, add other product lines, begin to sell in new or foreign markets, your sales should increase. How much is hard to say, but you have some idea of the goals.

• What are industry trends? No boom lasts forever. No bust does either.

• What are the economic trends in your markets and in the more general economy? Reading newspapers (*The Wall Street Journal* or the major city dailies), magazines (*Business Week, Forbes* and so on) and books helps. Keeping alert pays off and helps you understand the context in which your business plan unfolds.

Don't make the optimistic error of thinking you can spot the turns immediately and base your plans on that assumption. You can spot the turns in a general sense and be prepared to take advantage of them, but it is risky to count on a wisdom nobody else has ever maintained. Even the experts are occasionally mistaken.

• What competitive, technological or other factors will be likely during the forecast period?

The long-range forecasting process is simpler than for the one-year forecasts:

Annual sales by year

	Yr 1 (most likely)	Yr 2	Yr 3	Yr 4	Yr 5
Old products					
A. _____	_____	_____	_____	_____	_____
B. _____	_____	_____	_____	_____	_____
C. _____	_____	_____	_____	_____	_____
D. _____	_____	_____	_____	_____	_____
E. _____	_____	_____	_____	_____	_____
New products					
X. _____	_____	_____	_____	_____	_____
Y. _____	_____	_____	_____	_____	_____
Z. _____	_____	_____	_____	_____	_____
TOTALS	_____	_____	_____	_____	_____

Example of five-year sales forecast

	Yr 1	Yr 2	Yr 3	Yr 4	Yr 5
Independent stores	80	100	130	170	220
Chain stores	175	200	230	265	300
Individual (direct)	30	35	40	45	50
Government	90	100	100	100	100
Banks	30	30	50	70	70
Foreign	45	60	60	70	70
Other	15	15	15	15	15
TOTALS	465	540	625	735	845

Notes: Independent stores: Growth at ≈ 30% per year. Slight leveling off during Yr 2, while new lines are developed and the acquisition get integrated into business. This may be understated.

Chain stores: Anticipate 15% annual growth. There are some chains which we've just begun to approach; they may afford faster growth than shown here.

Individual (direct): Slow, steady growth anticipated. We're learning how to do this better.

Government: These markets may have peaked, or be nearing a peak. Very vulnerable to economic downturns.

Banks: Will rebound strongly in two or three years.

Foreign: Slow growth after next year's spurt.

Other: Level.

These figures will be spread later. While you can do a "worst case/best case" analysis, the long-range forecasts will still be questionable. One important idea to hold in mind is that some of your old products, markets or profit centers will decay during this period and new ones will arise to take their place. All small businesses have to be continuously reinvented.

The example above is deliberately conservative. A conservative projection is a barrier against staffing up too soon. As a matter of policy, it is wiser to wait until you have no choice but to add staff or equipment rather than anticipate growth that never comes, or comes too late. If the pace picks up, revise the forecasts (and as noted earlier, the important forecasts are those for one year out or less).

Spreading the sales forecast

The most difficult part of the sales forecast is now over. Spreading the annual forecasts is a very simple process. If you have kept monthly sales figures for several years, you will usually find patterns emerging. There are definite patterns in most markets, reflecting the buying behaviors of various customers. These patterns vary little from one year to the next and can be used as a guide.

The process is this: For each major market or product line (as in the example below), list last year's sales for each month. Figure the percentage of annual sales for each month. Multiply that figure by projected sales to get projected monthly sales. If last year was anomalous, use average monthly sales for the past several years to establish a more normal pattern.

Monthly sales pattern (in 000s)

	Last yr sales	% of annual sales	Projected
Jan	36	10	47
Feb	21	6	28
Mar	28	8	37
Apr	28	8	37
May	36	10	47
June	22	6	28
Jul	22	6	28
Aug	28	8	37
Sep	28	8	37
Oct	57	16	74
Nov	22	6	28
Dec	28	8	37
TOTALS	356		465

Keep notes to support your forecast: Independent store, chain store and government sales patterns are similar. The other markets are erratic—but since independent store, chain store and government markets together constitute about 75% of total sales, use their sales pattern for the entire forecast. This simplifies the forecast without sacrificing accuracy.

Note that these figures are rounded off to the nearest $1,000. This is accurate enough and makes computation easier. Keep the percentage to whole numbers. Fractions of a percent are too fine a measure to be useful.

The process is this: For each major market or product line, list historical sales for each month. Figure the percentage of annual sales for each month. Multiply that figure by projected annual sales to arrive at projected monthly sales.

This can be made more complex. You may want to break out figures from two or three years back to provide a more stable monthly percentage of annual sales pattern. Or you may want more detail.

You must have some set of reasons to expect a different sales pattern than shown in past years. Perhaps you are being more aggressive, or your markets are changing. The historical method works best for stable, ongoing businesses who are growing at a predictable pace.

To figure quarterly projections for years two through five, simply add up the percentage for each quarter and apply it to the appropriate forecast. In the example, the pattern is that 24% of annual sales take place in 1Q (first quarter), 24% in 2Q, 22% in 3Q, and 30% in 4Q. We multiply the projected year two, three, four and five totals by these percentages to reach quarterly figures. Each first quarter thus represents 24% of projected annual sales, each second quarter 24%, each third quarter 22%, and each fourth quarter 30%.

Quarterly annual sales projections

	% Annual	Yr 2	Yr 3	Yr 4	Yr 5
1Q	24	130	150	175	200
2Q	24	130	150	175	200
3Q	22	120	135	160	185
4Q	30	160	190	225	260
TOTALS	100%	540	625	735	845

Figures are rounded off for ease in calculations. Since these are extrapolations of guesses and estimates, they are at best suspicious.

Transitional businesses excluding start-ups can use this historical method effectively. Transitions can upset customers and this has to be taken into account in spreading the sales, but over time the old pattern will re-emerge. Transitional businesses will be ongoing businesses once the transition is complete. Hence you can safely use the same quarterly projection method as ongoing businesses after the first year.

Start-ups have two choices. If you are beginning a business, sales (beyond a brief opening flurry) will usually build slowly and take over a year to mimic trade/industry patterns. Skew your figures accordingly. Your research pays a dividend here. If you have been fortunate and persistent enough to find a similar business which is two to five years old, press the owners or managers for information on their early sales patterns. They may share it with you. Sometimes your banker or accountant can help you locate this kind of information.

The other choice is to make a "best guesstimate" for the first three months and be prepared to change it as often as monthly. Your first year will not be typical of a mature business, but should build toward trade or industry patterns. If your business is a seasonal industry, you will be affected by that seasonality. At least you can expect strong seasonal sales when the industry season is strong, if (an important consideration) you have made your presence known to the markets you serve.

The length of the sales cycle is another factor to work in. If it takes months to complete a sale and your sales pipeline is empty, or nearly so, the sales pattern will be affected. You don't start out at 100% sales efficiency.

Projections for year two will begin to approach trade and industry patterns, subject to start-up problems which can spill over. For year three and beyond, you can use trade and industry patterns comfortably: you will have enough experience after a year of operations to generate newer and more accurate forecasts and will most likely begin to approximate the high end of your industry patterns. If you invest time and effort in planning your business, you certainly will be at the high end. Most small businesses are woefully undermanaged and are vulnerable to a canny competitor.

Fast-growth businesses have two sets of forecasts to spread, and the shapes should differ, partly based on seasonal/historical patterns, partly on the very different sales levels forecast. The immediate future may be similar, but after two or three months the pictures differ markedly. Fast growth overwhelms normal patterns, while the slow growth or even contraction of sales in the fallback scenario tends toward the average trade/industry picture.

Ask yourself:
- When will sales (probably) stall or hit the wall?
- Are others entering this market (these markets)?
- What are the leading indicators in our particular sales patterns?
- Where are our products on their life-cycle?

Fast growth is self-limiting. Coming up with a second supernova is tough, and few companies can do it. Even fewer are consistently able to generate fast-growth products. And even among these, few can fund the growth. Let's see: 3-M, IBM, and who else?

Extending your sales forecasts by quarter for years two through five is iffy. The sales patterns in fast growth are erratic and not easy to extrapolate. How long will you enjoy fast growth? When will the competition invade your turf or will you saturate and outgrow your markets? What will you do for an encore?

Part of the difficulty is psychological: we get used to whatever patterns our businesses operate in and generalize or extrapolate from that familiar pattern. It's easy to become fat and complacent. Entire societies do this and end up losing their competitive advantage over other societies. Good times are always followed by more normal times. Remember the Old Testament story of the seven fat years followed by seven lean years?

Chapter 3
Turning Sales Forecasts into Projected Profit & Loss Statements

Sales forecasts are useful in and of themselves, but their most important use is as the basis of projected profit and loss (P&L) and cash flow. These two projections lead directly to changes in the balance sheet, which can also be treated as a projection, albeit a derivative one. If you are going to use your projections to substantiate a financing proposal, a projected balance sheet is often required. To be on the safe side, have your accountant check your figures. Nothing deflates a proposal quite as thoroughly as projections that don't fit together.

The process now becomes relatively mechanical. Your sales forecast is the key. Sales affect all the expense items on the P&L, and that ripples into the cash flow.

Sales forecast ➡ P&L projection ➡ Cash flow pro forma

Keep notes as you prepare your projections. You will need a record of how or why you choose this figure or that one. As experience corrects your forecasts, it helps to review what gave rise to the disparities between projected and actual performance. There will be some totally unexpected forces that blow projections apart. More often the cause will be an accumulation of small changes, and as you become more experienced and knowledgeable, fewer of these will surprise you. Your annotated projections are much stronger guides than the bare numbers alone could be.

The P&L projection comes first. This is not arbitrary. The P&L provides the most widely used measures of how well a company is doing. If you aren't thoroughly familiar with the P&L and balance sheet, get a copy of Merrill Lynch's 30-page booklet "How to Read a Financial Report." It's free from any Merrill Lynch office.

The P&L shows how your business performs over a period of time. Make sure that your P&L follows standard formats, but keep in mind that its purpose is to reflect your business. It is not being prepared for your CPA's convenience, or to fit a computer program. You can always take the information from your P&L and reformat it to meet other needs. Your fundamental need is to have accurate information available when you need it. An overly detailed P&L will not meet your needs. You won't use it, for one thing. As part of information control, keep it simple.

Sample P&L format
(1) Gross sales revenues
(2) Returns and allowances
(3) Net sales revenues
(4) Cost of goods sold
(5) Gross margin/profit
(6) Other income
(7) Total receipts
(8) Operating expenses
    salaries/wages
    payroll taxes
    benefits
    space costs
    marketing expenses
    professional services
    amortization and depreciation
    miscellaneous
(9) Total operating expenses
(10) Other expenses
(11) Interest expense
(12) Total expenses
(13) Pre-tax profit (loss)
(14) Taxes
(15) Net profit (loss)

Explanation:
(1) Total sales for the period. This is an aggregate figure. You may want to break it out, or have a separate sales schedule that adds up to this aggregate number.
(2) Discounts and returns. Monitor for sales practices, product quality. Sudden increases in these accounts flash a major warning. Fluctuations may merely be a function of sales level, but have to be checked to ensure continued quality and customer satisfaction.
(3) Net sales. Gross sales minus discounts and returns.
(4) Cost of goods sold (COGS) includes cost of purchasing inventories and direct sales costs (commissions, royalties, direct labor). COGS is usually the largest variable

expense. In manufacturing companies, this provides the first measure of operating efficiency, and would be fairly detailed. Your accountant will help you determine the right amount of detail.

(5) Gross margin or gross profit. Net sales minus COGS.

(6) Non-operating income, such as profit on sale of a fixed asset. These are usually non-recurring items: returns on investments, legal claims, etc.

(8) Operating expenses, the costs of doing business. Most of these are fixed, others are semi-variable and a few are variable. The order they are presented in is less important than the thoroughness. For example:

Payroll expenses (includes salaries, taxes, benefits).

Space costs (includes rent, utilities, maintenance).

Professional services (principally legal and accounting).

Marketing expenses (includes advertising, trade show attendance, training, promotional expenses)

Amortization and depreciation.

Miscellaneous. If some expenses are trivial, lump them together. If miscellaneous expenses exceed some arbitrary percentage of sales, say, one percent, be prepared to break them out.

(9) The sum of all operating expenses. Highly predictable in part because small differences in (8) tend to balance out.

(10) Other expenses. These are non-operating expenses other than interest.

(11) Interest is the most familiar non-operating expense, and is such an important measure that it should be given a prominent display. You want to monitor this closely. So will your banker.

(13) You get taxed on this amount.

(14) Consult your accountant. Tax minimization is a job for a specialist, as there are over 35,000 pages in the tax codes. Don't waste your time trying to master them. You have a business to run.

(15) Net profit (loss). The bottom line. It represents the success or failure of the business.

The way you use your P&L projection will influence where you need more or less detail. The idea behind managing by the numbers is to measure performance against an objective standard, keeping trends and comparisons in mind. Your P&L projection is a set of internally generated standards that represent your best estimates of what your business will do over the period the projection covers.

Key numbers you want to keep special track of are sales, gross margin and pre-tax profit (loss). If any of these items diverge significantly from the projections, you can look further. If they are in line with projections, move on to other activities. Managing by the numbers is intended to help you manage more efficiently.

Sales have already been broken out by month. Spread the cost of goods sold next, or the variable operating expenses. The order is immaterial. The same method applies to all variable expenses. Variable expenses go up and down as sales go up and down, and are usually calculated as a percent of anticipated sales.

Other operating expenses are fixed, coming up the same each time. Fixed expenses (the "nut") crop up whether you have sales or not. These payments include rent, utilities, lease payments and the basic costs of running your business. Keeping fixed costs under firm control is an ongoing management problem, since you have to gear up for anticipated sales or lose potential business, but also have to keep the nut down or face the danger of runaway costs. For most of us, wages and salaries are the largest fixed-cost item. A full breakdown of fixed and variable expenses is presented in Ch 6, "Break-even Analysis."

The convention for fixed expenses is that they are spread evenly across the year. Unless you have a good reason (which you would annotate), take the total annual expense and divide by 12. This applies to insurance and legal and accounting expenses, even if you pay them quarterly or annually. Your accountant can help you set up these projected expenses.

Fixed expenses are fixed only within limits. As your business grows, you will need more employees, more space, more equipment and so forth, which in turn will drive up fixed expenses. Unfortunately, trimming fixed expenses in periods of slow sales is much more difficult than adding fixed expenses in good times. The general rule of thumb is never to increase these fixed expenses until you are forced. *Opportunity costs won't put you out of business, but too-high fixed expenses might.*

The figures in your projected P&L will be your operating standards, so it behooves you to proceed carefully. As a guideline, use your most recent P&L, even if it is last year's. You can always add to it as you go along or reorganize it to better fit your needs.

Use 13-column paper for spreading sales and expenses. Yes, you could use a computer. The value of 13-column paper is that you have all of the information right in front of you, while most computer screens show only a fraction of the P&L at one time. Once the preliminary spread is done (on 13-column paper), transfer it to the computer for fine-tuning and calculation. This gives you the best of both worlds: hard copy backup, plus the computational power of the computerized spreadsheet.

Your aim is to create a working model of what you want or expect your business to do. This is another reason to keep notes. As you track the numbers, you have reasons for the decisions and assumptions you make. You may forget these reasons as you plow through the projection process.

Be alert to timing. As you work through the P&L projection line by line, keep asking yourself what changes you want to make and when you plan to implement those changes. If you plan to move to more spacious quarters, when? What added costs are involved? What other expenses will be affected? If you will be mounting a major marketing program in the fall, you don't spread it through the entire year. You add it to the expected marketing expenses at the time you incur the expense. You may also be replacing one cost with another. You don't want to separate the expense from the period in which the expense was incurred.

If this seems confusing, don't lose heart. Get help. The really important thing about the projected P&L is that it embodies your ideas. Your CPA or other financial advisor can grind out the numbers for you. But you must understand how those numbers were arrived at or know where to find out.

One-Year P&L Projection

SALES REVENUE	Jan	Feb	Mar	Apr	May	Jun	Jul
Products	$47,000	$28,000	$37,000	$37,000	$47,000	$28,000	$28,000
Other	$1,000	$1,000	$1,000	$1,000	$1,000	$1,000	$1,000
Returns & allowances	($150)	($150)	($150)	($150)	($150)	($150)	($150)
TOTALS	$47,850	$28,850	$37,850	$37,850	$47,850	$28,850	$28,850
COST OF GOODS							
Production cost	$10,340	$6,160	$8,140	$8,140	$10,340	$6,160	$6,160
Licensing fees	$3,760	$2,240	$2,960	$2,960	$3,760	$2,240	$2,240
Commissions	$2,820	$1,680	$2,220	$2,220	$2,820	$1,680	$1,680
Contract labor	$470	$280	$370	$370	$470	$280	$280
Freight	$940	$560	$740	$740	$940	$560	$560
TOTALS	$18,330	$10,920	$14,430	$14,430	$18,330	$10,920	$10,920
GROSS MARGIN	$29,520	$17,930	$23,420	$23,420	$29,520	$17,930	$17,930
OPERATING EXPENSES							
Salaries etc.	$10,000	$10,000	$10,000	$10,000	$10,000	$12,000	$12,000
Rent & utilities	$1,250	$1,250	$1,250	$1,250	$1,250	$1,250	$1,250
Insurance	$150	$150	$150	$150	$150	$150	$150
Marketing & advertising	$7,050	$4,200	$5,550	$5,550	$7,050	$4,200	$4,200
Travel	$300	$300	$200	$200	$200	$1,000	$200
Meals & entertainment	$200	$200	$150	$150	$150	$750	$150
Professional fees	$200	$200	$200	$200	$200	$200	$200
Telephone	$600	$600	$600	$600	$600	$400	$400
Equipment leases	$350	$350	$350	$350	$350	$350	$350
Repairs & maintenance	$100	$100	$100	$100	$100	$100	$100
Amortization & depreciation	$300	$300	$300	$300	$300	$300	$300
Miscellaneous	$100	$100	$100	$100	$100	$100	$100
Interest expense	$300	$300	$300	$300	$300	$300	$300
TOTALS	$20,900	$18,050	$19,250	$19,250	$20,750	$21,100	$19,700
PRETAX PROFIT (LOSS)	$8,620	($120)	$4,170	$4,170	$8,770	($3,170)	($1,770)
Fed. taxes	$0	$0	$0	$0	$0	$0	$0
State taxes	$517	($7)	$250	$250	$526	($190)	($106)
CUM. P.T. PROF (LOSS)	$8,620	$8,500	$12,670	$16,840	$25,610	$22,440	$20,670
NET PROFIT (LOSS)	$8,103	($113)	$3,920	$3,920	$8,244	($2,980)	($1,664)

One-Year P&L Projection (cont.)

SALES REVENUE	Aug	Sep	Oct	Nov	Dec	TOTALS	% of Net Rev
Products	$37,000	$37,000	$74,000	$28,000	$37,000	$465,000	98%
Other	$1,000	$1,000	$1,000	$1,000	$1,000	$12,000	3%
Returns & allowances	($150)	($150)	($150)	($150)	($150)	($1,800)	0.38%
TOTALS	$37,850	$37,850	$74,850	$28,850	$37,850	$475,200	100%
COST OF GOODS							
Production cost	$8,140	$8,140	$16,280	$6,160	$8,140	$102,300	22%
Licensing fees	$2,960	$2,960	$5,920	$2,240	$2,960	$37,200	8%
Commissions	$2,220	$2,220	$4,440	$1,680	$2,220	$27,900	6%
Contract labor	$370	$370	$740	$280	$370	$4,650	1%
Freight	$740	$740	$1,480	$560	$740	$9,300	2%
TOTALS	$14,430	$14,430	$28,860	$10,920	$14,430	$181,350	38%
GROSS MARGIN	$23,420	$23,420	$45,990	$17,930	$23,420	$293,850	62%
OPERATING EXPENSES							
Salaries etc.	$12,000	$12,000	$12,000	$12,000	$12,000	$134,000	28%
Rent & utilities	$1,250	$1,250	$1,250	$1,250	$1,250	$15,000	3%
Insurance	$150	$150	$150	$150	$150	$1,800	0%
Marketing & advertising	$5,550	$5,550	$11,100	$4,200	$5,550	$69,750	15%
Travel	$200	$500	$500	$500	$300	$4,400	1%
Meals & entertainment	$150	$400	$400	$400	$400	$3,500	1%
Professional fees	$200	$200	$200	$200	$200	$2,400	1%
Telephone	$400	$800	$800	$700	$600	$7,100	1%
Equipment leases	$350	$350	$350	$350	$350	$4,200	1%
Repairs & maintenance	$100	$100	$100	$100	$100	$1,200	0%
Amortization & depreciation	$300	$300	$300	$300	$300	$3,600	1%
Miscellaneous	$100	$100	$100	$100	$100	$1,200	0%
Interest expense	$300	$300	$300	$300	$300	$3,600	1%
TOTALS	$21,050	$22,000	$27,550	$20,550	$21,600	$251,750	53%
PRETAX PROFIT (LOSS)	$2,370	$1,420	$18,440	($2,620)	$1,820	$42,100	9%
Fed. taxes	$0	$0	$0	$0	$0	$0	0%
State taxes	$142	$85	$1,106	($157)	$109	$2,526	1%
CUM. P.T. PROF (LOSS)	$23,040	$24,460	$42,900	$40,280	$42,100		
NET PROFIT (LOSS)	$2,228	$1,335	$17,334	($2,463)	$1,711	$39,574	8%

One-year P&L projection

The following notes explain my reasoning as I project the P&L for an ongoing business shown on the preceding two pages. Whenever you put a forecast or projection together, the notes are an important part of the total package. Make sure that the decisions behind the projections are available if you need them. You don't have to share them with your investors, but you should have them available for your own purposes. Over time, they provide a valuable resource of ideas, reasoning, arguments over goals and direction.

The example is simplified; the level of detail you choose is up to you. Work with your accountant to decide what goes into your projections, and what level of detail suits your business best. In my company, we prepare a P&L forecast for each of three product lines. We are fully computerized, which makes monthly (or more frequent) comparisons of projected or budgeted and actual performance easy. Furthermore, we also prepare year-to-date (YTD) P&Ls for each product line, as well as a set of monthly and YTD P&Ls for the company as a whole. We use this amount of detail because it works for us. We could get by with less; we've seen companies who use more.

Notes to one-year P&L

Product sales are entered the month booked. They could all come in on the first or last day of the month. There are some instances when you might wish to break sales down by different periods, but in most cases monthly forecasts are sufficient.

Note that sales may or may not be cash received. While there is truth in the old saw "it's not a sale until you get paid," for purposes of the P&L most businesses operate on the accrual system. Some businesses have to do this for tax purposes. In this example, the sales pattern is derived from actual experience. If you don't have a history, the patterns still will be skewed for most businesses; knowing when and how people buy your product or service is important information.

Other revenue comes from non-product sales (consulting or installation fees, and so on). Not a major source of revenue but well worth having. In the example business, these fees come up erratically and upredictably but average $12,000/year.

Returns and allowances is an adjustment to gross sales revenues. A store might buy fifty boxes of gumdrops and return one box for credit. If returns and allowances are an important factor in your business, work returns and allowances into your forecast, although you need to know your gross sales revenue as a basis for ordering or production.

Experience with the market in the example shows a returns and allowance rate of less than 0.5%. Since our returns trickle in at a fairly uniform rate, the example is spread at ($150)/month. Note that this is a negative figure.

Both the erratic and unpredictable "other" revenue and the fairly stable "returns" are spread evenly throughout the year. Over time, if patterns did develop, they would be spread by those patterns. If it doesn't make a lot of difference how you spread an item, do it the easiest way: divide by 12.

NET SALES REVENUES. Gross sales revenues after returns and allowances have been subtracted.

COST OF GOODS SOLD (COGS). One of the most important figures for running your business. Some professional and other services have extremely low COGS, as they sell time rather than a product and might only include a few items they sell their clients. A hairdresser who sells brushes and shampoos would have a COGS; a hairdresser who only sells haircuts and styling would not. Check with your accountant. The breakdown of COGS in the example is as follows:

Production costs average 22% of sales. In analyzing cash flow, the timing of how subcontractors get paid is examined. For the P&L projection, this is figured at 25% of revenue (rounded to the nearest $100) to reflect the performance of the business.

Licensing fees (to the inventor of the product) average 8% of sales.

Commissions are paid to sales representatives, which averages six percent of sales. This is an expense you'd like to see go up. If your sales reps prosper, so do you.

Contract labor is rimarily part-time help. One percent of sales.

Freight, a surprisingly large sum, part of which can be billed out to customers. Averages two percent of sales.

GROSS MARGIN is the most important single figure to this point, as it is what pays the operating expenses and provides a margin for profit.

OPERATING EXPENSES. The proverbial nut. Most of these fixed expenses come due monthly.

Salaries, etc. Salaries plus payroll taxes plus benefits (which run about 25% of salaries). Although actual pay periods vary, this example is figured as if each month were the same. In June some raises are expected which will carry through for the rest of the year.

Space costs. Rent and utilities, paid at a flat rate.

Insurance. Paid quarterly, but the expense is spread monthly.

Marketing. This large expense, although exhaustively analyzed in most companies as a percentage of sales, is treated as a fixed expense. It includes advertising and all sales promotion, such as catalogs, flyers, brochures, point-of-sale displays, product samples and trade shows. The costs are accrued sporadically, but the benefits accrue steadily. Although this is a variable, treat it as a fixed expense for budgeting purposes on the theory that you have invested heavily to gain a market presence and will fight to retain it. Even if sales are down you'd continue to fund this item at the projected rate. If possible, you'd invest more than budgeted.

Travel. Varies with season, and is tied to sales calls and trade shows. Attendance at a major trade show causes the aberration in the example.

Meals and entertainment. Meetings with customers and attending trade shows.

Professional fees. Paid twice a year, benefit accrues throughout. Primarily for accounting and maintaining legal status (keeping the corporation registered and so on).

Telephone. Heaviest before fall selling season.

Equipment and leases. Electronic whizbangs (computers and workstations).

Repairs and maintenance. Keeping premises tidy, machinery working.

Amortization and depreciation. Write-off over time of money invested in equipment. Used to lower taxable income. Depreciation writes down the cost of tangible assets, while amortization does the same for intangible assets such as goodwill. Accountants revel in this item; it provides them with a chance to show off. Some experts swear that amortization and depreciation is the last, best tax loophole.

Miscellaneous. Office supplies, miscellaneous postage. Odds and ends.

Interest expense. On loans for equipment and working capital. Note that this is interest only. The repayment of principal shows up on the cash-flow budget.

PRE-TAX PROFIT (LOSS). A measure of the efficiency of the business. This is a better measure than the after-tax profit or loss. Your tax burden is largely a function of your accountant's skill. Be glad you're making a profit to be taxed on. Be worried if you are not.

Federal tax. Corporate income tax. Due to a carry-forward of losses from previous years, no tax is due in year 1.

State tax. In some states, no breaks here, even if previous years generated a loss. Odd but true.

CUMULATIVE PRETAX PROFIT (LOSS). Use to compare this year's performance to historical data. Spot trends. See Ch 8, "Variance Analysis."

Governing rules in preparing a P&L forecast

• Don't sweat the small stuff. While you want to be accurate, there is a point of diminishing returns you reach quickly. Don't agonize over spreading a minor item such as the telephone bill, which is part variable, part fixed.

• On large numbers, think it through. That's why the sales forecast is so detailed. You are trying to establish major guidelines. You can't include everything. Just as a baseball manager looks first at the batting averages, ERAs, won/loss record and the like before turning to finer measures, you want to be able swiftly to check your company's progress. That means riding herd on revenues, gross margin and pretax profit or loss.

• If you have a computer, use it. The 13-column pad is wonderful as an aid to thought. The computer is terrific for grinding out the calculations, sparing you much of the drudgery of spreadsheet analysis.

• Customize your P&L to your own uses. For some entries, one line is more informative than six. Greater detail doesn't always lead to better information. Quite the opposite often holds true.

• Your projected P&Ls should have the same format and entries as your monthly P&L. Otherwise you'll waste time shuffling numbers from the monthlies to some other format. If this kind of work is routine for your bookkeeper, use of fisCAL™ or other spreadsheet analyzers is an excellent idea.

• Once you get the hang of making a projection, the actual time involved is minimal. The effort before the projection is where time mounts up, as you think through the initial goals and sales forecasts. Perhaps 90% of your time will be spent on these initial steps.

Second- to fifth-year P&L projection

Use the one-year-by-month projection to run your business. Use the two- to five-year quarterly projection as a polestar to keep you more or less on course as you strive to reach long-term objectives. You revise the one-year forecast every six months or so (more often in cases of transitional or fast-growth businesses), so in a sense you never implement the long-range projections. They keep receding, still serving their useful and important heuristic function, but never being actually applied.

Quarterly projections for years two through five (and their annotation) are similar to the monthly projection. The main difference is detail. Five-year forecasts are much less detailed, essentially an extrapolation of past and current growth, tempered as always by your knowledge and experience. The five-year forecast is built on sales forecasts (see Ch 2), which themselves are extrapolations and estimates of what will probably happen. Don't get swamped in details. In particular, operating expenses should be made as simple as possible.

Notes to four-year P&L

Product sales include "other" and come from the five-year sales forecast in Ch 2. Don't break out anticipated unit sales in exaggerated detail.

Returns: one half of one percent of sales.

COGS is usually sensitive to volume: the longer the production run, the lower the unit cost, and over the next few years we will be able to benefit from longer production runs.

Production cost is figured at 22% of sales, the true historic figure.

Licensing fees: 8% of sales.

Commissions: 6% of sales.

Contract labor: 1% of sales.

Freight: 2% of sales.

Salaries/wages includes benefits and payroll taxes. This line will grow ≈ 10% per year, to cover both raises and new or added personnel. We'll continue to run a lean crew, however.

Marketing: 15% of gross sales.

Other operating expenses (everything else except interest) will increase at 6% per year.

Interest increase anticipated in mid-year 3 (additional debt for growth).

Federal income taxes. Can't avoid them forever. Figured at 15% of pretax profit.

State taxes: 6% of pretax profit.

You can sometimes defer taxes by deferring revenues, but eventually you have to pay them. You hope you do because that means you are continuing to be profitable in spite of growth.

P&L Projection Years Two to Five

	YEAR TWO					YEAR THREE				
	1Q	2Q	3Q	4Q	TOTALS	1Q	2Q	3Q	4Q	TOTALS
SALES REVENUE										
Products	$130	$130	$120	$160	$540	$150	$150	$135	$190	$625
Other	$0	$0	$0	$0	$0	$0	$0	$0	$0	$0
Returns and allowances	($1)	($1)	($1)	($1)	($3)	($1)	($1)	($1)	($1)	($3)
TOTALS	$129	$129	$119	$159	$537	$149	$149	$134	$189	$622
COST OF GOODS										
Production costs	$29	$29	$26	$35	$119	$33	$33	$30	$42	$138
Licensing fees	$10	$10	$10	$13	$43	$12	$12	$11	$15	$50
Commissions	$8	$8	$7	$10	$32	$9	$9	$8	$11	$38
Contract labor	$1	$1	$1	$2	$5	$2	$2	$1	$2	$6
Freight	$3	$3	$2	$3	$11	$3	$3	$3	$4	$13
TOTALS	$51	$51	$47	$62	$211	$59	$59	$53	$74	$244
GROSS MARGIN	$79	$79	$73	$97	$327	$91	$91	$82	$115	$378
OPERATING EXPENSES										
Salaries & benefits	$40	$40	$40	$40	$160	$44	$44	$44	$44	$176
Marketing & advertising	$20	$20	$18	$24	$81	$23	$23	$20	$29	$94
Other operating expense	$11	$11	$11	$11	$44	$12	$12	$12	$12	$48
Interest expense	$1	$1	$1	$1	$4	$1	$1	$2	$2	$6
TOTALS	$72	$72	$70	$76	$289	$80	$80	$78	$87	$324
PRETAX PROFIT (LOSS)	$7	$7	$3	$21	$38	$11	$11	$3	$28	$54
Federal taxes	$1	$1	$0	$3	$6	$2	$2	$1	$4	$8
State taxes	$0	$0	$0	$1	$2	$1	$1	$0	$2	$3
CUM P.T. PR (LOSS)	$7	$14	$17	$38		$11	$23	$26	$54	$109
NET PROFIT (LOSS)	$6	$6	$2	$16	$30	$9	$9	$3	$22	$43

P&L Projection Years Two to Five (cont.)

	YEAR FOUR					YEAR FIVE				
	1Q	2Q	3Q	4Q	TOTALS	1Q	2Q	3Q	4Q	TOTALS
SALES REVENUE										
Products	$175	175	$160	$225	$735	$200	$200	$185	$260	$845
Other	$0	$0	$0	$0	$0	$0	$0	$0	$0	$0
Returns and allowances	($1)	($1)	($1)	($1)	($4)	($1)	($1)	($1)	($1)	($4)
TOTALS	$174	$174	$159	$224	$731	$199	$199	$184	$259	$841
COST OF GOODS										
Production costs	$39	$39	$35	$50	$162	$44	$44	$41	$57	$186
Licensing fees	$14	$14	$13	$18	$59	$16	$16	$15	$21	$68
Commissions	$11	$11	$10	$14	$44	$12	$12	$11	$16	$51
Contract labor	$2	$2	$2	$2	$7	$2	$2	$2	$3	$8
Freight	$4	$4	$3	$5	$15	$4	$4	$4	$5	$17
TOTALS	$68	$68	$62	$88	$287	$78	$78	$72	$101	$330
GROSS MARGIN	$106	$106	$97	$136	$445	$121	$121	$112	$157	$511
OPERATING EXPENSES										
Salaries & benefits	$48	$48	$48	$48	$192	$53	$53	$53	$53	$212
Marketing & advertising	$26	$26	$24	$34	$110	$30	$30	$28	$39	$127
Other operating expense	$13	$13	$13	$13	$52	$14	$14	$14	$14	$56
Interest expense	$2	2	$2	$2	$8	$2	$2	$2	$2	$8
TOTALS	$89	$89	$87	$97	$362	$99	$99	$97	$108	$403
PRETAX PROFIT (LOSS)	$17	$17	$10	$39	$82	$22	$22	$15	$49	$108
Federal taxes	$2	$2	$1	$6	$12	$3	$3	$2	$7	$16
State taxes	$1	$1	$1	$2	$5	$1	$1	$1	$3	$7
CUM P.T. PR (LOSS)	$17	$33	$43	$82		$22	$44	$59	$108	
NET PROFIT (LOSS)	$13	$13	$8	$31	$65	$17	$17	$12	$39	$86

Chapter 4
Cash Flow Pro Forma

The cash flow projection (pro forma budget) is the most important single statement for controlling your business. A cash budget controls the dribbles that bleed a business: an unnecessary purchase here, an unwise hire there, a small donation to a worthy cause. The dribbles soon amount to a gusher, and plugging that outflow is extraordinarily difficult.

A well-prepared cash flow budget is all you need to run your business profitably. All the other managerial tools (the P&L, balance sheet, ratio analyses and strategic analyses) are secondary. They can enhance and improve profitability only if you have positive cash flow. Once cash flow turns negative, you won't have time to fiddle with ratios or worry about profitability. You'll spend all your time trying to plug the leaks and achieve positive cash flow.

Mr. Micawber put it best in *David Copperfield*: "Annual income twenty pounds, annual expenditure nineteen six, result happiness. Annual income twenty pounds, annual expenditure twenty pounds ought and six, result misery." Dickens was right. He understood cash flow. In essence, "happiness is a positive cash flow." Fred Adler, a prominent venture capitalist, went so far as to have T-shirts printed with this motto. You can also say "positive cash flow equals survival," at least temporarily, for small business. In the long run you must make an operating profit (the main source of cash), but at least in the short run cash flow is more important.

Cash flow is concerned with money in motion, the actual flow of cash through your business. While the P&L is modified to a degree by timing, in cash flow budgeting timing is all-important. When does a sale turn into cash? When does a bill get paid? When do you receive a loan, proceeds of a new investment? The underlying questions are: When? How much?

Managing cash

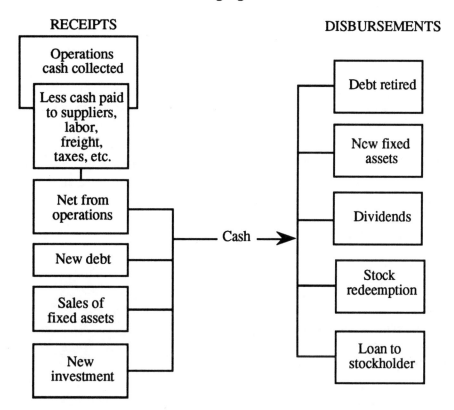

Cash flow sketch

1. Cash at beginning of period
Add revenues
2. Sales of products to be collected currently
3. Cash to be received from other sources
4. Cash received from prior period sales
5. Cash received from assets sold
6. Cash received from loans
8. Cash from bad debts recovered
9. Miscellaneous cash received
Total cash received
Subtract expenses
10. New inventory purchased
11. Salaries/wages to be paid
12. Fringe benefits to be paid
13. New equipment to be purchased
   14. Processing equipment
   15. Office, sales equipment
   16. Transportation equipment
17. Insurance
18. Fees
   19. Accounting

20. Legal
21. Utilities
22. Telephone
   23. Heat, light, power
   24. Advertising
25. Principal and interest on debt
26. Transportation
   27. Oil, gas
   28. Vehicle maintainence
   29. Tires
30. Freight
31. Provision for bad debts
32. Taxes to be paid
   33. Income (state, federal)
   34. Property/excise
   35. Payroll
   36. Sales
37. Dividends to be paid, loans to stockholders
38. Provision for unforeseen contingency
Total cash received less total expenses equals
Cash at end of period

The mechanics of preparing your cash flow are not difficult, provided you have been realistic in your sales forecasting and P&L projections, which provide the basic matter to be expressed in your cash flow.

Cash flow starts with sales. Sales drive every business, and if you are going to raise new investment money, new debt or stay in business, you have to make an operating profit. This is only possible if sales revenues exceed expenses.

Managing by the numbers is simple: stick to what you know. Buy low, sell high. Keep expenses in line. Increase sales. Reinvest profits for growth. When we get too far from these basic precepts we get into trouble. A good cash flow takes work, but that work pays fat dividends in control and profitability.

You can get cash flow forms from your accountant, bank or the Small Business Administration. Modify them to fit your needs. They differ in minor detail, but basically they look like this:

Format of cash flow pro forma

    (1) Cash inflows:
        Cash sales
        Cash from receivables
        Other
    (2) Cash from operations (subtotal)
    (3) Proceeds of loan
    (4) New investment
    (5) Other
    (6) TOTAL CASH IN
    (7) Cash disbursements:
    (8) Variable disbursements
    (9) Fixed disbursements
    (10) Other
    (11) TOTAL CASH DISBURSEMENTS
    (12) Cash flow
    (13) Cumulative cash flow
    (14) Cash at start of period
       + Cash inflow
       – Cash outflow
       = Cash at end of period

Explanation

    (1) Cash inflows. All cash received from any operating source.

    (2) Cash from operations. This is the primary source of cash. The other sources are dependent on a steady flow of cash from operations, which is corrected for receivables timing. When we receive cash makes a big difference to most of us small business owners. Cash always comes in more slowly than we hope and flows out faster. If all of your sales are cash sales, you can focus on the disbursements (after copying the sales forecast month by month). For the majority of businesses, however, extending credit to customers is a

fact of life. If your customers buy from you now and pay you later this pattern must be reflected in your cash flow.

The "other" sources of operating cash can be anything from secondary cash sources (proceeds of investments, interest on deposit accounts being common) to refunds of taxes. Tax refunds can be significant sources of cash, but you have to have made the payment in the first place.

(3) Loans and (4) investments. You borrow money, cash comes in. You or someone else invests in the business, cash comes in.

(5) Other. Includes sales of fixed assets, proceeds of lawsuits settled in your favor, or other non-operating cash inflows.

(6) Total cash in: Sum of (2) through (5). All cash inflows for the period.

(7) Cash disbursements don't equal expenses. Disbursements involve the cash you actually shell out (amount and timing). You may incur an expense but take your time about paying it. You don't disburse any cash until you send the check.

(8) Variable disbursements correspond to the variable expenses on the P&L. You enter them as they are actually paid, not before. You have considerable latitude in when to make your payments, subject to the good will and tolerance of your suppliers and other creditors.

(9) Fixed disbursements correspond to fixed expenses. This is the nut, the cash that you pay out no matter how high or low sales are. This does not include amortization and depreciation or non-cash expenses.

(10) Other disbursements. Variable and fixed costs are operating expenses transmogrified into disbursements. "Other" includes any other non-operating use of cash: loans to stockholders, dividends, stock repurchase, principal payments on loans or purchase of fixed assets are examples.

(11) Total cash outflows equal the sum of (8), (9) and (10). All cash outflows for the period.

(12) Cash flow = (6) Cash inflows – (11) Cash outflows. If this figure is positive, you enjoy positive cash flow. If it is negative, you suffer negative cash flow.

(13) Cumulative cash flow: add current month cash flow to the sum of the previous months' cash flows.

Some forms add a space for "cash flow from operations." However, very few small businesses use this kind of analysis, as non-operating inflows and disbursements tend to be rare, small, or both. Loans are usually for operating purposes such as inventory or equipment, and lawsuit awards are unusual.

Projecting a cash flow involves the usual conflict between detail and overload. You want to make sure the sales forecast, recast in the cash flow, is accurate, but you don't want to bog down in too much fine tuning. One way to strike a reasonable balance is to keep track of the average age of receivables. Except for start-ups, which require guesswork to a large extent, this comes from the balance sheet and P&L:

Net sales average + trade receivables = number of receivables turns per year

365   ÷ receivables turn = average age of receivables

Thus if sales were $356,000, and receivables averaged $20,000, there would be 17.8 turns, for an average of 21 days. In other words, non-cash sales turn to cash, on average, 21 days later:

$$356/20 = 17.8 \text{ (turns)}$$

$$365/17.8 = 21 \text{ (days)}$$

Figuring timing on sales

(1) Annual sales	$_____
(2) Average receivables	$_____
(3) Total credit sales (average receivables) times 12	= $_____
(4) Receivables turn (annual sales)/(average receivables)	= _____ times
(5) Average age of receivables 365/(Receivables turn)	= _____ days
(6) Percentage of credit sales (Total credit sales)/(Annual sales)	= _____ %
(7) Percent of cash sales 100% minus (Percentage of credit sales)	= _____ %

As an example of how to use this form, here is how the figures we will use in the cash flow budgeting example are derived:

(1) Annual sales		$356,000
(2) Average receivables		$ 20,000
(3) Total credit sales (average receivables) times 12	=	$240,000
(4) Receivables turn (annual sales)/(average receivables)	=	17.8 times
(5) Average age of receivables 365/(Receivables turn)	=	20.5 days
(6) Percentage of credit sales (Total credit sales)/(Annual sales)	=	67%
(7) Percent of cash sales 100% minus (Percentage of credit sales)	=	33%

Credit and collection patterns tend to be stable. Since you'll be tracking receivables anyway, you may find that you already have a good grasp of the age and importance of your receivables (see Ch 9, "Ratios," for more). Following our example, one third of each month's forecasted sales will come in as cash in the month booked, the remainder in the following month. While the average age is 20 days, I would suggest a little slack. Receivables have a nasty habit of growing old and I'd want to be conservative. Total December sales in the previous year were $28,000, of which two thirds turned to cash in January.

Look at **Cash flow worksheet 1**. The accuracy of the numbers is spurious; it comes from applying a mechanical formula to the sales forecast (the memo figures at the top): one third goes into cash sales, two thirds is deferred one month. Since I am using a computerized spreadsheet, I'll let them ride. If I were doing this by hand, I'd round off to the nearest $1,000.

You might wonder if the next step would be to add whatever numbers might be appropriate for new debt or new investment. The answer depends on how you plan to use the cash flow. If the new debt or new investment is already secure (preferably in hand), the answer is yes. You would want to measure its impact on your cash flow.

Otherwise the answer would be no. You want to get a line on your operating cash needs, including capital, and the very best way to do this is to work through your variable and fixed disbursements next. This will allow you to figure when you'll hit a negative cash position and decide how to resolve the problem.

In cash flow worksheet 1, total cash from operations is $458,970, while sales for the same period are forecast as $465,000. The difference is due to revenue coming in from the previous December ($18,760) and being deferred from the following December ($24,970). The difference is $6,030, which corresponds to the difference between forecasted sales and forecasted cash from operations.

Cash flow worksheet 1

(Memo sales figures)						
$28,000	$47,000	$28,000	$37,000	$37,000	$47,000	$28,000

	Jan	Feb	Mar	Apr	May	Jun
CASH INFLOWS						
Cash sales	$15,510	$9,240	$12,210	$12,210	$15,510	$9,240
Cash from receivables	$18,760	$31,490	$18,760	$24,790	$24,790	$31,490
Other						
Total cash from operations	$34,270	$40,730	$30,970	$37,000	$40,300	$40,730
New investment						
New debt						
Sale of fixed assets						
TOTAL CASH INFLOWS	$34,270	$40,730	$30,970	$37,000	$40,300	$40,730

							TOTALS
(Memo sales figures)	$28,000	$37,000	$37,000	$74,000	$28,000	$37,000	$465,000

	Jul	Aug	Sep	Oct	Nov	Dec	
CASH INFLOWS							
Cash sales	$9,240	$12,210	$12,210	$24,420	$9,240	$12,210	$153,450
Cash from receivables	$18,760	$18,760	$24,790	$24,790	$49,580	$18,760	$305,520
Other							
Total cash from operations	$28,000	$30,970	$37,000	$49,210	$58,820	$30,970	$458,970
New investment							
New debt							
Sale of fixed assets							
TOTAL CASH INFLOWS	$28,000	$30,970	$37,000	$49,210	$58,820	$30,970	$458,970

Now to the cash disbursement side of the equation. The easiest place to start is with fixed disbursements, since they can easily be isolated and entered. These are absolutely predictable disbursements, with fixed amounts and timing. Some of the figures will be rounded off. The aim is to present an accurate picture of the entire company's cash flow, with special accuracy of the larger cash items.

Notes to cash flow worksheet 2

Salaries. In the P&L, this included benefits and payroll taxes. For purposes of projecting cash flow, more detail is handy. It is all to easy to screw up taxes—easy and expensive. Withheld taxes are included in salaries, which have been rounded off to reflect pay schedules. March and October have three pay periods; the rest have two pay periods.

Payroll taxes. FUTA, plus employer's share of FICA, other taxes on salaries or wages.

Benefits. Primarily health insurance, employees' share FICA.

Utilities. Higher in winter, lower in summer.

Insurance. Semi-annual premium.

Marketing & advertising. Keep this figure on a cash basis (see the P&L projection) as it is paid as incurred. While this obscures some of the cash flow of actual marketing and advertising disbursements, some of the disbursements can be arranged to suit your convenience. The actual marketing and advertising figures are budgeted separately. Too much detail would serve no purpose here; the variables for travel, meals and entertainment are shown on the next two lines.

Professional fees. Paid quarterly.

Telephone. Pay 30 days after receiving service.

Equipment leases. Payments on leased equipment.

Repairs & maintenance. Goes up and down; too small to schedule.

Miscellaneous. Petty cash items.

Quarterly principal and interest payments, loan 1. This is a payment of $1,800 for interest only on a subordinated loan: $12,000 at 15%, payable to the lender.

Monthly principal and interest payments, loan 2. A $20,000 loan for equipment. The terms are 12% for 5 years. Monthly payments will total $1,200 interest, $4,200 principal this year.

Other. Leave this line blank for now. Once you have completed your cash flow, you will know what you have to finance (and when you need financing). At that time, we will return to this line. It exemplifies use of the cash flow in managing by the numbers. If you plan to buy a fixed asset or make any capital investment, this is where you would put the proposed expenditure.

The next step in preparing a cash-flow budget is to spread the variable disbursements. This is where your knowledge of your business and industry is really tested. Since we are interested in when these disbursements are made as well as the amounts, we can't simply multiply cash inflows from operations by an even percentage each month except in the limiting case of an all-cash business. Presenting COGS in a separate schedule helps some business owners; you may not want or need this level of detail, or might find a greater degree of accuracy important.

Cash flow worksheet 2

(Memo sales figures)						
$28,000	$47,000	$28,000	$37,000	$37,000	$47,000	$28,000

	Jan	Feb	Mar	Apr	May	Jun
CASH INFLOWS						
Cash sales	$15,510	$9,240	$12,210	$12,210	$15,510	$9,240
Cash from receivables	$18,760	$31,490	$18,760	$24,790	$24,790	$31,490
Other	$850	$850	$850	$850	$850	$850
Total cash from operations	$35,120	$41,580	$31,820	$37,850	$41,150	$41,580
New Investment						
New debt						
Sale of fixed assets						
TOTAL CASH INFLOWS	$35,120	$41,580	$31,820	$37,850	$41,150	$41,580
CASH DISBURSEMENTS						
VARIABLE DISBURSEMENTS						
Production costs						
Licensing fees						
Commissions						
Contract labor						
Freight						
Total cost of goods sold	$0	$0	$0	$0	$0	$0
Travel						
Meals & entertainment						
TOTAL VARIABLE	$0	$0	$0	$0	$0	$0
FIXED DISBURSEMENTS						
Salaries	$7,000	$7,000	$10,500	$7,000	$7,000	$8,000
Payroll taxes	$700	$700	$1,050	$700	$700	$800
Benefits	$1,750	$1,750	$2,625	$1,750	$1,750	$2,000
Rent	$1,000	$1,000	$1,000	$1,000	$1,000	$1,000
Utilities	$300	$300	$300	$250	$250	$200
Insurance	$900					$900
Marketing & advertising	$7,050	$4,200	$5,550	$5,550	$7,050	$4,200
Professional fees			$600			$600
Telephone	$600	$600	$600	$600	$600	$600
Equipment leases	$300	$300	$300	$300	$300	$300
Repairs & maintenance	$100	$100	$100	$100	$100	$100
Miscellaneous	$100	$100	$100	$100	$100	$100
TOTAL FIXED	$19,800	$16,050	$22,725	$17,350	$18,850	$18,800
Principal & Interest: Loan 1			$450			$450
Principal & Interest: Loan 2	$450	$450	$450	$450	$450	$450
Other (describe)						
TOTAL LOANS & OTHER	$450	$450	$900	$450	$450	$900
TOTAL CASH DISBURSEMENTS	$20,250	$16,500	$23,625	$17,800	$19,300	$19,700
CASH FLOW						
CUMULATIVE CASH FLOW						
OPERATING CASH FLOW						
STARTING CASH						
+CASH INFLOWS						
- CASH DISBURSEMENTS						
ENDING CASH POSITION						

Cash flow worksheet 2 (cont.)

(Memo sales figures)							TOTALS
	$28,000	$37,000	$37,000	$74,000	$28,000	$37,000	$465,000
	Jul	**Aug**	**Sep**	**Oct**	**Nov**	**Dec**	
CASH INFLOWS							
Cash sales	$9,240	$12,210	$12,210	$24,420	$9,240	$12,210	$153,450
Cash from receivables	$18,760	$18,760	$24,790	$24,790	$49,580	$18,760	$305,520
Other	$850	$850	$850	$850	$850	$850	$10,200
Total cash from operations	$28,850	$31,820	$37,850	$50,060	$59,670	$31,820	$469,170
New Investment							$0
New debt							$0
Sale of fixed assets							$0
TOTAL CASH INFLOWS	$28,850	$31,820	$37,850	$50,060	$59,670	$31,820	$469,170
CASH DISBURSEMENTS							
VARIABLE DISBURSEMENTS							
Production costs							$0
Licensing fees							$0
Commissions							$0
Contract labor							$0
Freight							$0
Total Cost of goods sold	$0	$0	$0	$0	$0	$0	$0
Travel							$0
Meals & entertainment							$0
TOTAL VARIABLE	$0	$0	$0	$0	$0	$0	$0
FIXED DISBURSEMENTS							
Salaries	$8,000	$8,000	$8,000	$12,000	$8,000	$8,000	$98,500
Payroll taxes	$800	$800	$800	$1,200	$800	$800	$9,850
Benefits	$2,000	$2,000	$2,000	$3,000	$2,000	$2,000	$24,625
Rent	$1,000	$1,000	$1,000	$1,000	$1,000	$1,000	$12,000
Utilities	$200	$200	$250	$250	$300	$300	$3,100
Insurance							$1,800
Marketing & advertising	$4,200	$5,550	$5,550	$11,100	$4,200	$5,550	$69,750
Professional fees			$600			$600	$2,400
Telephone	$400	$400	$400	$800	$800	$700	$7,100
Equipment leases	$300	$300	$300	$300	$300	$300	$3,600
Repairs & maintenance	$100	$100	$100	$100	$100	$100	$1,200
Miscellaneous	$100	$100	$100	$100	$100	$100	$1,200
TOTAL FIXED	$17,100	$18,450	$19,100	$29,850	$17,600	$19,450	$235,125
Principal & Interest: Loan 1			$450			$450	$1,800
Principal & Interest: Loan 2	$450	$450	$450	$450	$450	$450	$5,400
TOTAL OTHER	$450	$450	$900	$450	$450	$900	$7,200
TOTAL CASH DISBURSEMENTS	$17,550	$18,900	$20,000	$30,300	$18,050	$20,350	$242,325
CASH FLOW							
CUMULATIVE CASH FLOW							
OPERATING CASH FLOW							
STARTING CASH							
+CASH INFLOWS							
- CASH DISBURSEMENTS							
ENDING CASH POSITION							

Cash flow worksheet 3

(Memo sales figures)

	$28,000	$47,000	$28,000	$37,000	$37,000	$47,000	$28,000
		Jan	Feb	Mar	Apr	May	Jun
CASH INFLOWS							
Cash sales		$15,510	$9,240	$12,210	$12,210	$15,510	$9,240
Cash from receivables		$18,760	$31,490	$18,760	$24,790	$24,790	$31,490
Other		$850	$850	$850	$850	$850	$850
Total cash from operations		$35,120	$41,580	$31,820	$37,850	$41,150	$41,580
New Investment							
New debt							
Sale of fixed assets							
TOTAL CASH INFLOWS		$35,120	$41,580	$31,820	$37,850	$41,150	$41,580
CASH DISBURSEMENTS							
VARIABLE DISBURSEMENTS							
Production costs		$9,075	$21,175		$6,975	$16,275	
Licensing fees							$17,920
Commissions		$5,294			$6,511		
Contract labor		$470	$280	$370	$370	$470	$280
Freight		$940	$560	$740	$740	$940	$560
Total cost of goods sold		$15,779	$22,015	$1,110	$14,596	$17,685	$18,760
Travel		$300	$300	$200	$200	$200	$1,000
Meals & entertainment		$200	$200	$150	$150	$150	$750
TOTAL VARIABLE		$16,279	$22,515	$1,460	$14,946	$18,035	$20,510
FIXED DISBURSEMENTS							
Salaries		$7,000	$7,000	$10,500	$7,000	$7,000	$8,000
Payroll taxes		$700	$700	$1,050	$700	$700	$800
Benefits		$1,750	$1,750	$2,625	$1,750	$1,750	$2,000
Rent		$1,000	$1,000	$1,000	$1,000	$1,000	$1,000
Utilities		$300	$300	$300	$250	$250	$200
Insurance		$900					$900
Marketing & advertising		$7,050	$4,200	$5,550	$5,550	$7,050	$4,200
Professional fees				$600			$600
Telephone		$600	$600	$600	$600	$600	$600
Equipment leases		$300	$300	$300	$300	$300	$300
Repairs & maintenance		$100	$100	$100	$100	$100	$100
Miscellaneous		$100	$100	$100	$100	$100	$100
TOTAL FIXED		$19,800	$16,050	$22,725	$17,350	$18,850	$18,800
Principal & Interest: Loan 1				$450			$450
Principal & Interest: Loan 2		$450	$450	$450	$450	$450	$450
Other (describe)							
TOTAL LOANS & OTHER		$450	$450	$900	$450	$450	$900
TOTAL CASH DISBURSEMENTS		$36,529	$39,015	$25,085	$32,746	$37,335	$40,210
CASH FLOW							
CUMULATIVE CASH FLOW							
OPERATING CASH FLOW							
STARTING CASH							
+CASH INFLOWS							
- CASH DISBURSEMENTS							
ENDING CASH POSITION							

Cash flow worksheet 3 (cont.)

(Memo sales figures)							TOTALS
	$28,000	$37,000	$37,000	$74,000	$28,000	$37,000	$465,000
	Jul	**Aug**	**Sep**	**Oct**	**Nov**	**Dec**	
CASH INFLOWS							
Cash sales	$9,240	$12,210	$12,210	$24,420	$9,240	$12,210	$153,450
Cash from receivables	$18,760	$18,760	$24,790	$24,790	$49,580	$18,760	$305,520
Other	$850	$850	$850	$850	$850	$850	$10,200
Total cash from operations	$28,850	$31,820	$37,850	$50,060	$59,670	$31,820	$469,170
New Investment							$0
New debt							$0
Sale of fixed assets							$0
TOTAL CASH INFLOWS	$28,850	$31,820	$37,850	$50,060	$59,670	$31,820	$469,170
CASH DISBURSEMENTS							
VARIABLE DISBURSEMENTS							
Production costs	$10,425	$24,325		$10,575	$24,675		$123,500
Licensing fees						$18,560	$36,480
Commissions	$7,235			$5,911			$24,952
Contract labor	$280	$370	$370	$740	$280	$370	$4,650
Freight	$560	$740	$740	$1,480	$560	$740	$9,300
Total cost of goods sold	$18,500	$25,435	$1,110	$18,706	$25,515	$19,670	$198,882
Travel	$200	$200	$500	$500	$500	$300	$4,400
Meals & entertainment	$150	$150	$400	$400	$400	$400	$3,500
TOTAL VARIABLE	$18,850	$25,785	$2,010	$19,606	$26,415	$20,370	$206,782
FIXED DISBURSEMENTS							
Salaries	$8,000	$8,000	$8,000	$12,000	$8,000	$8,000	$98,500
Payroll taxes	$800	$800	$800	$1,200	$800	$800	$9,850
Benefits	$2,000	$2,000	$2,000	$3,000	$2,000	$2,000	$24,625
Rent	$1,000	$1,000	$1,000	$1,000	$1,000	$1,000	$12,000
Utilities	$200	$200	$250	$250	$300	$300	$3,100
Insurance							$1,800
Marketing & advertising	$4,200	$5,550	$5,550	$11,100	$4,200	$5,550	$69,750
Professional fees			$600			$600	$2,400
Telephone	$400	$400	$400	$800	$800	$700	$7,100
Equipment leases	$300	$300	$300	$300	$300	$300	$3,600
Repairs & maintenance	$100	$100	$100	$100	$100	$100	$1,200
Miscellaneous	$100	$100	$100	$100	$100	$100	$1,200
TOTAL FIXED	$17,100	$18,450	$19,100	$29,850	$17,600	$19,450	$235,125
Principal & Interest: Loan 1			$450			$450	$1,800
Principal & Interest: Loan 2	$450	$450	$450	$450	$450	$450	$5,400
TOTAL OTHER	$450	$450	$900	$450	$450	$900	$7,200
TOTAL CASH DISBURSEMENTS	$36,400	$44,685	$22,010	$49,906	$44,465	$40,720	$449,107
CASH FLOW							
CUMULATIVE CASH FLOW							
OPERATING CASH FLOW							
STARTING CASH							
+CASH INFLOWS							
- CASH DISBURSEMENTS							
ENDING CASH POSITION							

Notes to cash flow worksheet 3

Production costs average 22% of sales. The figures in the top line are the forecasted sales figures, so these amounts will reflect those sales. The timing is a different matter. Production runs are quarterly. Subcontractors are paid 30% on signing the work order, 70% on completion. To avoid running out of stock, this business tries to keep one to two months ahead. Accordingly, in January they start production going for anticipated sales in March, April and May. In February they pay the balance. In March they have no production disbursements. In April the cycle begins again. (Sales for January and February next year are $65,000 and $39,000 respectively. At least that's the goal.)

Production costs are the largest cash disbursements in operations. Watch it carefully. The Law of Large Numbers (Version A) says to pay attention to the big numbers first and in greater detail than the smaller numbers.

Licensing fees are paid twice a year. The formula averages 8% of cumulative sales less a 10% holdback against returns, but as returns are low the holdback washes out. This is paid in June and December, for sales in the prior six months; that is, December through May, June through November. (Bankers aren't the only ones to profit on float.) Last December's sales were $28,000.

Try to stagger license-fee payments and production costs and make sure both don't fall due in the same month. This smooths out the cash flow, and represents the fundamental cash-flow balance that successful cash-flow managers strive to reach.

Commissions are paid quarterly for the preceding three months. The rate is 6% of cash from operations. A receivable has to be paid before the sales representatives get their commissions, which encourages them to handle credit sales wisely. If they generate a lot of returns, they don't get rewarded for it.

Contract labor is tied to sales, is erratically paid, and amounts to about one percent of net sales. Because it is relatively steady, we spread it by formula: one percent per month times sales.

Freight charges are directly related to sales levels. Two percent of each month's sales (roughly) goes to freight.

This ends the COGS section. Keep in mind that the patterns and percentages are idiosyncratic. They fit this operation, and are based on a particular set of experiences. Even if you were in the same business, your patterns and percentages would differ. There would be a strong family resemblance, however, in that many of the practices will be common.

Travel, meals and entertainment are considered variable disbursements but don't have a regular percentage of sales as their base. Instead, they are tied to ongoing activities and occasional major trade shows. These are "plugged in" figures based on estimated outlays.

At this stage our cash flow budget is almost finished. All of the major disbursements, both fixed and variable, have been identified.

Cash flow worksheet 4

(Memo sales figures)						
$28,000	$47,000	$28,000	$37,000	$37,000	$47,000	$28,000
	Jan	**Feb**	**Mar**	**Apr**	**May**	**Jun**
CASH INFLOWS						
Cash sales	$15,510	$9,240	$12,210	$12,210	$15,510	$9,240
Cash from receivables	$18,760	$31,490	$18,760	$24,790	$24,790	$31,490
Other	$850	$850	$850	$850	$850	$850
Total cash from operations	$35,120	$41,580	$31,820	$37,850	$41,150	$41,580
New Investment						
New debt						
Sale of fixed assets						
TOTAL CASH INFLOWS	$35,120	$41,580	$31,820	$37,850	$41,150	$41,580
CASH DISBURSEMENTS						
VARIABLE						
Production costs	$9,075	$21,175		$6,975	$16,275	
Licensing fees						$17,920
Commissions	$5,294			$6,511		
Contract labor	$470	$280	$370	$370	$470	$280
Freight	$940	$560	$740	$740	$940	$560
Total cost of goods sold	$15,779	$22,015	$1,110	$14,596	$17,685	$18,760
Travel	$300	$300	$200	$200	$200	$1,000
Meals & entertainment	$200	$200	$150	$150	$150	$750
TOTAL VARIABLE	$16,279	$22,515	$1,460	$14,946	$18,035	$20,510
FIXED						
Salaries	$7,000	$7,000	$10,500	$7,000	$7,000	$8,000
Payroll taxes	$700	$700	$1,050	$700	$700	$800
Benefits	$1,750	$1,750	$2,625	$1,750	$1,750	$2,000
Rent	$1,000	$1,000	$1,000	$1,000	$1,000	$1,000
Utilities	$300	$300	$300	$250	$250	$200
Insurance	$900					$900
Marketing & advertising	$7,050	$4,200	$5,550	$5,550	$7,050	$4,200
Professional fees			$600			$600
Telephone	$600	$600	$600	$600	$600	$600
Equipment leases	$300	$300	$300	$300	$300	$300
Repairs & maintenance	$100	$100	$100	$100	$100	$100
Miscellaneous	$100	$100	$100	$100	$100	$100
TOTAL FIXED	$19,800	$16,050	$22,725	$17,350	$18,850	$18,800
Principal & Interest: Loan 1			$450			$450
Principal & Interest: Loan 2	$450	$450	$450	$450	$450	$450
TOTAL LOANS	$450	$450	$900	$450	$450	$900
TOTAL CASH DISBURSEMENTS	$36,529	$39,015	$25,085	$32,746	$37,335	$40,210
CASH FLOW	($1,409)	$2,565	$6,735	$5,104	$3,815	$1,370
CUMULATIVE CASH FLOW	($1,409)	$1,156	$7,891	$12,994	$16,809	$18,179
OPERATING CASH FLOW	($959)	$3,015	$7,635	$5,554	$4,265	$2,270
STARTING CASH	$8,500	$7,091	$9,656	$16,391	$21,494	$25,309
+CASH INFLOWS	$35,120	$41,580	$31,820	$37,850	$41,150	$41,580
- CASH DISBURSEMENTS	$36,529	$39,015	$25,085	$32,746	$37,335	$40,210
ENDING CASH POSITION	$7,091	$9,656	$16,391	$21,494	$25,309	$26,679

Cash flow worksheet 4 (cont.)

	Jul	Aug	Sep	Oct	Nov	Dec	TOTALS
(Memo sales figures)	$28,000	$37,000	$37,000	$74,000	$28,000	$37,000	$465,000
CASH INFLOWS							
Cash sales	$9,240	$12,210	$12,210	$24,420	$9,240	$12,210	$153,450
Cash from receivables	$18,760	$18,760	$24,790	$24,790	$49,580	$18,760	$305,520
Other	$850	$850	$850	$850	$850	$850	$10,200
Total cash from operations	$28,850	$31,820	$37,850	$50,060	$59,670	$31,820	$469,170
New Investment							$0
New debt							$0
Sale of fixed assets							$0
TOTAL CASH INFLOWS	$28,850	$31,820	$37,850	$50,060	$59,670	$31,820	$469,170
CASH DISBURSEMENTS							
VARIABLE							
Production costs	$10,425	$24,325		$10,575	$24,675		$123,500
Licensing fees						$18,560	$36,480
Commissions	$7,235			$5,911			$24,952
Contract labor	$280	$370	$370	$740	$280	$370	$4,650
Freight	$560	$740	$740	$1,480	$560	$740	$9,300
Total cost of goods sold	$18,500	$25,435	$1,110	$18,706	$25,515	$19,670	$198,882
Travel	$200	$200	$500	$500	$500	$300	$4,400
Meals & entertainment	$150	$150	$400	$400	$400	$400	$3,500
TOTAL VARIABLE	$18,850	$25,785	$2,010	$19,606	$26,415	$20,370	$206,782
FIXED							
Salaries	$8,000	$8,000	$8,000	$12,000	$8,000	$8,000	$98,500
Payroll taxes	$800	$800	$800	$1,200	$800	$800	$9,850
Benefits	$2,000	$2,000	$2,000	$3,000	$2,000	$2,000	$24,625
Rent	$1,000	$1,000	$1,000	$1,000	$1,000	$1,000	$12,000
Utilities	$200	$200	$250	$250	$300	$300	$3,100
Insurance							$1,800
Marketing & advertising	$4,200	$5,550	$5,550	$11,100	$4,200	$5,550	$69,750
Professional fees			$600			$600	$2,400
Telephone	$400	$400	$400	$800	$800	$700	$7,100
Equipment leases	$300	$300	$300	$300	$300	$300	$3,600
Repairs & maintenance	$100	$100	$100	$100	$100	$100	$1,200
Miscellaneous	$100	$100	$100	$100	$100	$100	$1,200
TOTAL FIXED	$17,100	$18,450	$19,100	$29,850	$17,600	$19,450	$235,125
Principal & Interest: Loan 1			$450			$450	$1,800
Principal & Interest: Loan 2	$450	$450	$450	$450	$450	$450	$5,400
TOTAL LOANS	$450	$450	$900	$450	$450	$900	$7,200
TOTAL CASH DISBURSEMENTS	$36,400	$44,685	$22,010	$49,906	$44,465	$40,720	$449,107
CASH FLOW	($7,550)	($12,865)	$15,840	$154	$15,205	($8,900)	$20,063
CUMULATIVE CASH FLOW	$10,630	($2,235)	$13,605	$13,758	$28,963	$20,063	
OPERATING CASH FLOW	($7,100)	($12,415)	$16,740	$604	$15,655	($8,000)	$27,263
STARTING CASH	$26,679	$19,130	$6,265	$22,105	$22,258	$37,463	$8,500
+CASH INFLOWS	$28,850	$31,820	$37,850	$50,060	$59,670	$31,820	$469,170
- CASH DISBURSEMENTS	$36,400	$44,685	$22,010	$49,906	$44,465	$40,720	$449,107
ENDING CASH POSITION	$19,130	$6,265	$22,105	$22,258	$37,463	$28,563	$28,563

Notes to cash flow worksheet 4

Cash flow is arrived at by subtracting cash disbursements from cash inflows (line 17 minus line 53). In the example, cash flow is negative in January, July, August and
December, otherwise positive. It is positive for the total year.

Cumulative cash flow, Jan + Feb + Mar + … + Dec. The cumulative cash flow tends to
balance out the inevitable slopping about of some of the figures. It goes up and down,
hits a negative figure in August and rebounds strongly in the fourth quarter. This fits
the sales and revenue patterns of this business. By knowing in advance that sales will
be down in August, the management can plot a strategy to minimize the impact.
Perhaps a loan, or asking for a prepayment, or additional capital, or letting a bill slide
over a bit? Remember the 3% slack in production costs? Through August, that totals
$2,648, enough to cover the negative figure. That's a good example of how to use the
preliminary cash flow.

Operating cash flow is figured by subtracting variable and fixed disbursements from cash
from operations. This cleans out non-operating sources and uses of cash and provides
an operating cash budget. Many business owners find this an especially helpful figure
and also prepare a similar operating P&L budget. The aim is to answer the question of
whether operations are generating or eating cash. You hope for generation of cash, as it
is the engine that drives your business.

The last four lines project your cash position, based on cash flow. The example company
started the year with $8,500 on hand and would end up with $28,000+. In real life, this
wouldn't be allowed to happen. The cash would be reinvested in the business to generate growth, retire debt, purchase new equipment or other fixed assets. Or parked temporarily in an interest-bearing deposit account.

Five-year cash flow projections

Long range cash-flow projections are less useful than the P&L five-year projections.
Their main use is to help identify capital needs if the short-term (one-year) cash flow has
not turned positive. For most businesses the main reason to prepare a long term cash-flow
projection is to satisfy investor or banker demands. It can also be used to understand the
potential impact on the company of major investments or divestitures; most financial proposals include a three- or five-year cash-flow pro forma to show how an investment will
pay off. Your accountant or other financial advisors should help you make sure that the
numbers hang together, but once again, it is your ideas and insights that are expressed (or
should be) in five-year projections.

If you need to prepare long range cash-flow projections, follow this procedure:

1. Start with the long range P&L forecast. This contains most of the information needed
in preparing your cash flow quarterlies for years two through five.

2. As in the earlier cash flow projection, the cash inflows will consist of cash sales,
conversion of accounts receivable to cash, new investment, new debt, and the proceeds of
the sale of fixed assets. The timing of the first two is less critical than in the one-year pro
forma because most receivables, for most companies, don't stretch out much beyond 90

days—that is, all sales become cash within the quarter. If you have an erratic sales pattern and a long receivables turn your particular timing has to be shown.

3. Timing of new debt, new equity investment, or the proceeds of sales of fixed assets (including sale of a division or profit center) is very important. Long-range plans, particularly if they will be used to raise new capital, focus on the impact of such cash inflows. The long-term P&L forecast will show how they affect profitability. The cash-flow pro forma shows how the plan will be implemented and liquidity problems avoided.

4. On the disbursement side, the fixed-versus-variable distinctions remain important, but less detail need be shown. The three or five-year pro forma is not concerned with minutia. While considerable detail is necessary in the one-year pro forma because it will be used as a budget, the long-term concern is just this: will the company become liquid under the assumptions underlying the pro forma?

5. Keep notes. Whether or not the plans are implemented, the notes will help you understand your business better.

In the example that follows, a quarterly cash flow projection for years two through five, the assumptions are similar to those of the quarterly P&L projections: steady growth, no dramatic changes.

Notes to quarterly cash flow projection

Cash from operations reflects cash in from sales. Since the average account receivable is 20 days old, this simplifies the projection. There would be some slippage if the major sales months (January, May and October) fell at the end of their respective quarters. As it is, all sales will turn to cash.

Variable and fixed disbursements come from the attached displays, which are used to minimize clutter. When it is necessary to turn the projection into a budget, more detail would be added.

Cash flow is positive and growing each year, which affords a measure of comfort. The disbursements have been slightly inflated, inflows slightly reduced.

Schedule A:

Production costs for the first quarter of year one includes an extra month's production to make further calculation simpler. Last year (year one pro forma) took account of production for December through February. By adding March to second-quarter totals, the first-quarter production costs are inflated, but thereafter each quarter's production covers the next quarter's inventory.

Licensing fees and commissions have also been jiggled to make calculation simpler. Licensing fees ordinarily are for the preceding six months; I added in December of year one sales to the first and second quarter totals to put them on a biannual basis. This distorts the realities a bit by moving payments ahead, an inherently conservative measure. The same applies to sales commissions.

Schedule B:

Fixed disbursements. Salaries advance 10% per year, including taxes and benefits. Rent remains stable at $12,000 per year. The other disbursements grow at six percent per year (more or less).

Quarterly cash flow projections, years two through five

					TOTALS
(Memo sales figures)	$130	$130	$120	$160	$540
Year 2	**1Q**	**2Q**	**3Q**	**4Q**	
CASH INFLOWS					
Cash from operations	$130	$130	$120	$160	$540
New investment					$0
New debt					$0
Sale of fixed assets					$0
TOTAL CASH INFLOWS	$130	$130	$120	$160	$540
VARIABLE DISBURSEMENTS					
(from Schedule A)	$69	$88	$66	$96	$319
FIXED DISBURSEMENTS					
(from Schedule B)	$48	$48	$48	$48	$193
Principal & Interest: loans	$2	$1	$2	$2	$7
Principal & Interest: new loan					$0
Other (describe)		Equipment	$20		$20
TOTAL LOANS & OTHER	$2	$1	$22	$2	$27
TOTAL CASH DISBURSEMENTS	$119	$138	$136	$146	$539
CASH FLOW	$11	($8)	($16)	$14	$1
CUMULATIVE CASH FLOW	$11	$4	($13)	$1	
OPERATING CASH FLOW	$11	($8)	($16)	$14	
STARTING CASH		$11	$4	($13)	
+CASH INFLOWS	$130	$130	$120	$160	
- CASH DISBURSEMENTS	$119	$138	$136	$146	
ENDING CASH POSITION	$11	$4	($13)	$1	

SCHEDULE A: VARIABLE DISBURSEMENTS					
Production costs	$34	$26	$35	$33	$129
Licensing fees		$24		$22	$46
Commissions	$8	$12	$7	$10	$36
Contract labor	$1	$1	$1	$2	$5
Freight	$3	$3	$2	$3	$11
Total cost of goods sold	$46	$66	$46	$70	$228
Marketing & advertising	$20	$20	$18	$24	$81
Travel	$2	$2	$1	$1	$6
Meals & entertainment	$1	$1	$1	$1	$4
TOTAL VARIABLE	$69	$88	$66	$96	$319

SCHEDULE B: FIXED DISBURSEMENTS	
Salaries	$160
Payroll taxes	
Benefits	
Rent	$12
Utilities	$3
Insurance	$2
Professional fees	$2
Telephone	$8
Equipment leases	$4
Repairs & maintenance	$1
Miscellaneous	$1
TOTAL FIXED	$193
QUARTERLY DISBURSEMENTS	$48

Quarterly cash flow projections, years two through five (cont.)

					TOTALS
(Memo sales figures)	$150	$150	$135	$190	$625
Year 3	**1Q**	**2Q**	**3Q**	**4Q**	
CASH INFLOWS					
Cash from operations	$150	$150	$135	$190	$625
New investment					
New debt			$20		
Sale of fixed assets					
TOTAL CASH INFLOWS	$150	$150	$155	$190	$645
VARIABLE DISBURSEMENTS					
(from Schedule A)	$72	$95	$77	$114	$358
FIXED DISBURSEMENTS					
(from Schedule B)	$53	$53	$53	$53	$210
Principal & Interest: loans	$2	$2	$1	$2	$7
Principal & Interest: new loan			$2		$2
Other (describe)					
TOTAL LOANS & OTHER	$2	$2	$3	$2	$9
TOTAL CASH DISBURSEMENTS	$127	$149	$133	$169	$577
CASH FLOW	$24	$1	$22	$21	$68
CUMULATIVE CASH FLOW	$24	$24	$47	$68	
OPERATING CASH FLOW	$24	$1	$2	$21	$48
STARTING CASH		$24	$24	$47	
+CASH INFLOWS	$150	$150	$155	$190	
- CASH DISBURSEMENTS	$127	$149	$133	$169	
ENDING CASH POSITION	$24	$24	$47	$68	
SCHEDULE A: VARIABLE DISBURSEMENTS					
Production costs	$33	$30	$42	$39	$143
Licensing fees		$24		$26	$50
Commissions	$9	$9	$8	$11	$38
Contract labor	$2	$2	$1	$2	$6
Freight	$3	$3	$3	$4	$13
Total cost of goods sold	$47	$67	$54	$82	$249
Marketing & advertising	$23	$23	$20	$29	$94
Travel	$2	$3	$2	$2	$9
Meals & entertainment	$1	$2	$1	$2	$6
TOTAL VARIABLE	$72	$95	$77	$114	$358
SCHEDULE B: FIXED DISBURSEMENTS					
Salaries	$176	44	$44	$44	$308
Payroll taxes					
Benefits					
Rent	$12				
Utilities	$3				
Insurance	$3				
Professional fees	$2				
Telephone	$8				
Equipment leases	$4				
Repairs & maintenance	$1				
Miscellaneous	$1				
TOTAL FIXED	$210				
QUARTERLY DISBURSEMENTS	$53				

Quarterly cash flow projections, years two through five (cont.)

					TOTALS
(Memo sales figures)	$175	$175	$160	$225	$735
Year 4	**1Q**	**2Q**	**3Q**	**4Q**	**TOTAL**
CASH INFLOWS					
Cash from operations	$175	$175	$160	$225	$735
New investment					
New debt					
Sale of fixed assets					
TOTAL CASH INFLOWS	$175	$175	$160	$225	$735
VARIABLE DISBURSEMENTS					
(from Schedule A)	$85	$110	$91	$133	$418
FIXED DISBURSEMENTS					
(from Schedule B)	$57	$57	$57	$57	$228
Principal & Interest: loans	$2	$2	$1	$2	$7
Principal & Interest: new loan	$2		$2		$4
Other (describe)					$0
TOTAL LOANS & OTHER	$4	$2	$3	$2	$11
TOTAL CASH DISBURSEMENTS	$146	$169	$151	$192	$657
CASH FLOW	$30	$6	$9	$33	$78
CUMULATIVE CASH FLOW	$30	$35	$44	$78	
OPERATING CASH FLOW	$30	$6	$9	$33	$78
STARTING CASH		$35	$50	$93	
+CASH INFLOWS	$175	$175	$160	$225	
- CASH DISBURSEMENTS	$146	$169	$151	$192	
ENDING CASH POSITION	$30	$41	$59	$126	
SCHEDULE A: VARIABLE DISBURSEMENTS					
Production costs	$39	$35	$50	$44	$167
Licensing fees		$28		$31	$59
Commissions	$11	$11	$10	$14	$44
Contract labor	$2	$2	$2	$2	$7
Freight	$4	$4	$3	$5	$15
Total cost of goods sold	$54	$79	$64	$95	$292
Marketing & advertising	$26	$26	$24	$34	$110
Travel	$2	$3	$2	$2	$9
Meals & entertainment	$2	$2	$1	$2	$7
TOTAL VARIABLE	$85	$110	$91	$133	$418
SCHEDULE B: FIXED DISBURSEMENTS					
Salaries	$192	$48	$48	$48	$336
Payroll taxes					
Benefits					
Rent	$12				
Utilities	$3				
Insurance	$3				
Professional fees	$3				
Telephone	$9				
Equipment leases	$4				
Repairs & maintenance	$1				
Miscellaneous	$1				
TOTAL FIXED	$228				
QUARTERLY DISBURSEMENTS	$57				

Quarterly cash flow projections, years two through five (cont.)

(Memo sales figures)					TOTALS
	$200	$200	$185	$260	$845
				Jan Yr 6 =	$230
Year 5	**1Q**	**2Q**	**3Q**	**4Q**	
CASH INFLOWS					
Cash from operations	$200	$200	$185	$260	$845
New investment					
New debt					
Sale of fixed assets					
TOTAL CASH INFLOWS	$200	$200	$185	$260	$845
VARIABLE DISBURSEMENTS					
(from Schedule A)	$96	$125	$106	$153	$479
FIXED DISBURSEMENTS					
(from Schedule B)	$63	$63	$63	$63	$252
Principal & Interest: loans	$2	$2	$1	$2	$7
Principal & Interest: new loan	$2		$2		$4
Other (describe)					
TOTAL LOANS & OTHER	$4	$2	$3	$2	$11
TOTAL CASH DISBURSEMENTS	$163	$190	$172	$218	$742
CASH FLOW	$37	$10	$13	$42	$103
CUMULATIVE CASH FLOW	$37	$47	$61	$103	
OPERATING CASH FLOW	$37	$10	$13	$42	$103
STARTING CASH		$47	$71	$127	
+CASH INFLOWS	$200	$200	$185	$260	
- CASH DISBURSEMENTS	$163	$190	$172	$218	
ENDING CASH POSITION	$37	$58	$84	$169	

SCHEDULE A: VARIABLE DISBURSEMENTS

	1Q	2Q	3Q	4Q	TOTALS
Production costs	$44	$41	$57	$51	$193
Licensing fees		$32		$36	$68
Commissions	$12	$12	$11	$16	$51
Contract labor	$2	$2	$2	$3	$8
Freight	$4	$4	$4	$5	$17
Total cost of goods sold	$62	$91	$74	$110	$336
Marketing & advertising	$30	$30	$28	$39	$127
Travel	$2	$2	$2	$2	$8
Meals & entertainment	$2	$2	$2	$2	$8
TOTAL VARIABLE	$96	$125	$106	$153	$479

SCHEDULE B: FIXED DISBURSEMENTS

	1Q	2Q	3Q	4Q	TOTALS
Salaries	$212	$53	$53	$53	$371
Payroll taxes					
Benefits					
Rent	$12				
Utilities	$4				
Insurance	$4				
Professional fees	$4				
Telephone	$10				
Equipment leases	$4				
Repairs & maintenance	$1				
Miscellaneous	$1				
TOTAL FIXED	$252				
QUARTERLY DISBURSEMENTS	$63				

Using the cash flow projection

The cash flow projection provides monthly cash budget figures, which if well-based are the best standards you can have to help you manage your business. If you pick up nothing else from this book than how to set standards and try to achieve them, you'll be in better shape than most businesses.

One of the most important uses of the cash-flow budget, especially for start-ups and businesses in transition, is to establish capital needs. It is the best way to anticipate financing needs, including when to prepare proposals to present to banks, or to help investors (yourself included) reach decisions. Use this early-warning system to build your credibility with your banker. A timely proposal will invariably be better received than a panicky request for funds, right now, to meet payroll or cover taxes.

For start-ups and transitional businesses

Capital needs are roughly determined by the magnitude of negative cash flow. As you either start or redirect a business, you will face periods of negative cash flow and must have a strategy in place to counteract those outflows.

Most small businesses are undercapitalized. We all hope to generate enough operating profit to grow our way out of under-capitalization (by retaining earnings), but this is usually not possible. Growth eats cash faster than it generates cash, so except for the patient (or the fortunate: you may have major customers who will fund your growth by prepayment), more capital will be required. Bankers watch the debt-to-worth ratio closely, so financing your way through start-up or transition may not be possible. As a rule of thumb, a debt-to-worth ratio in excess of 2:1 will shut off new credit. (See Ch 9, "Ratios," for more on this.)

That leaves invested capital as the primary source of funds. How much capital do you need and when will you need it? If your projections show a substantial cumulative negative cash flow and the monthly cash flows have not turned positive, continue the cash flow projection until your business shows a consistent positive cash flow. *If your pro formas go out more than two years with consistently negative or only sporadically positive cash flows, sit down with your advisors. Your business plans must change or you should shut the doors now and avoid future failure.* This is extraordinarily valuable advice to heed. Remember: survival equals positive cash flow.

If the periods of negative cash flow are of a shorter duration, and the cumulative cash flow is positive, the cash-flow projection will show you when to borrow, how much, and when and how you can pay it back without creating further cash-flow problems. Look to the timing and amount of the cash flows. Ask your banker to help you determine the proper kind of credit to seek (line of credit, or receivables or inventory financing, or other). Bankers spend a lot of time learning how to finance small businesses, and your banker should be able to explain his or her reasoning.

Just having a cash-flow pro forma will bathe your business in a favorable light. The cash-flow projections (and the quarterlies for the next few years) illuminate seasonal credit needs and point out the need for additional working capital, which can often be financed by a bank.

Doubling rule of capital

Tom Weber, president of CFO Associates of Lexington, Massachusetts, asserts that getting proper capitalization (especially equity, since the debt windows are harder to open these days) is the toughest problem for most small businesses, especially those which are growing steadily but slowly. He quotes a Boston venture capitalist, Bob Crowley: "The Golden Rule? Those who have the gold rule...." Tom says make your cash-flow projection, find the low point, then triple it. He adds that on his first projection he uses the information provided by the company's executives, then on the second pass questions costs line by line, and on the third pass goes to great lengths to make the assumptions explicit.

If the cash flow is positive within 12–18 months, look at the point of the greatest negative cumulative cash flow. Double this figure. That's the minimum amount of new capital needed.

Why double? Because whatever can go wrong will go wrong. You may find that a smaller amount will suffice or a combination of invested capital and debt or reserved capital will see you through, but it is prudent to line up cash while you can.

Note that all this is extremely rough. I've assumed that you already know what the trade averages are, for a business doing your (forecasted or actual) sales level, and have a business net worth that is in the ballpark. This rule of thumb helps determine the additional capital needed.

For fast-growth businesses

Fast-growth businesses devour cash, pile up receivables and run the risk of becoming illiquid. For such a business, there are only two possibilities: slow down growth to harvest the profits from the sales, or get new investment into the business fast. The latter is normally the better route to pursue (unless a sales slowdown won't invite hungry competitors), but the amounts needed require a more sophisticated approach. Fortunately, if this is your problem, there are plenty of experts to help you calculate your capital needs.

You would use the cash-flow projections (including quarterlies) to ascertain credit needs the same way any other business would. The difference is that your cash flow will undergo especially severe scrutiny, as the sums tend to be greater and the risks more substantial than in the other scenarios. That's why you want to consult experts. The stakes are too large to learn as you go.

For ongoing businesses

For ongoing businesses, the cash-flow projection is the heart of any financing proposal. You may want to use your most optimistic scenario rather than your most conservative scenario as the basis, but the moves are basically the same:

• Negative cash flow calls for more equity, more debt or both, as well as some operational and strategic changes.

• Persistent negative cash flow is a cause for alarm. The path to bankruptcy is foreshadowed by persistent negative cash flow. At the very least, the business plan should be rewritten and all the assumptions rechecked.

• Look for amounts, timing and how the infusion of cash will be repaid.

Effect of slow sales on cash flow

	Jan	Feb	Mar	Apr	May	Jun	Jul
(Memo sales figures) $28,000	$40,000	$20,000	$30,000	$30,000	$34,000	$20,000	$28,000
CASH INFLOWS							
Cash sales	$13,200	$6,600	$9,900	$9,900	$11,220	$6,600	$9,240
Cash from receivables	$18,760	$26,800	$13,400	$20,100	$20,100	$22,780	$13,400
Other	$850	$850	$850	$850	$850	$850	$850
Total cash from operations	$32,810	$34,250	$24,150	$30,850	$32,170	$30,230	$23,490
New Investment							
New debt							
Sale of fixed assets							
TOTAL CASH INFLOWS	$32,810	$34,250	$24,150	$30,850	$32,170	$30,230	$23,490
CASH DISBURSEMENTS							
VARIABLE							
Production costs	$7,050	$16,450		$6,375	$14,875		$10,425
Licensing fees						$14,560	
Commissions	$5,294			$5,473			$5,595
Contract labor	$400	$200	$300	$300	$340	$200	$280
Freight	$800	$400	$600	$600	$680	$400	$560
Total cost of goods sold	$13,544	$17,050	$900	$12,748	$15,895	$15,160	$16,860
Travel	$300	$300	$200	$200	$200	$1,000	$200
Meals & entertainment	$200	$200	$150	$150	$150	$750	$150
TOTAL VARIABLE	$14,044	$17,550	$1,250	$13,098	$16,245	$16,910	$17,210
FIXED							
Salaries	$7,000	$7,000	$10,500	$7,000	$7,000	$8,000	$8,000
Payroll taxes	$700	$700	$1,050	$700	$700	$800	$800
Benefits	$1,750	$1,750	$2,625	$1,750	$1,750	$2,000	$2,000
Rent	$1,000	$1,000	$1,000	$1,000	$1,000	$1,000	$1,000
Utilities	$300	$300	$300	$250	$250	$200	$200
Insurance	$900					$900	
Marketing & advertising	$6,000	$3,000	$4,500	$4,500	$5,100	$3,000	$4,200
Professional fees			$600			$600	
Telephone	$600	$600	$600	$600	$600	$600	$400
Equipment leases	$300	$300	$300	$300	$300	$300	$300
Repairs & maintenance	$100	$100	$100	$100	$100	$100	$100
Miscellaneous	$100	$100	$100	$100	$100	$100	$100
TOTAL FIXED	$18,750	$14,850	$21,675	$16,300	$16,900	$17,600	$17,100
Principal & Interest: Loan 1			$450			$450	
Principal & Interest: Loan 2	$450	$450	$450	$450	$450	$450	$450
Other (describe)							
TOTAL LOANS & OTHER	$450	$450	$900	$450	$450	$900	$450
TOTAL CASH DISBURSEMENTS	$33,244	$32,850	$23,825	$29,848	$33,595	$35,410	$34,760
CASH FLOW	($434)	$1,400	$325	$1,002	($1,425)	($5,180)	($11,270)
CUMULATIVE CASH FLOW	($434)	$966	$1,291	$2,293	$868	($4,312)	($15,582)
OPERATING CASH FLOW	$16	$1,850	$1,225	$1,452	($975)	($4,280)	($10,820)
STARTING CASH	$8,500	$8,066	$9,466	$9,791	$10,793	$9,368	$4,188
+CASH INFLOWS	$32,810	$34,250	$24,150	$30,850	$32,170	$30,230	$23,490
- CASH DISBURSEMENTS	$33,244	$32,850	$23,825	$29,848	$33,595	$35,410	$34,760
ENDING CASH POSITION	$8,066	$9,466	$9,791	$10,793	$9,368	$4,188	($7,082)

Effect of slow sales on cash flow (cont.)

(Memo sales figures)						TOTALS
	$37,000	$37,000	$74,000	$28,000	$37,000	$415,000
	Aug	**Sep**	**Oct**	**Nov**	**Dec**	
CASH INFLOWS						
Cash sales	$12,210	$12,210	$24,420	$9,240	$12,210	$136,950
Cash from receivables	$18,760	$24,790	$24,790	$49,580	$18,760	$272,020
Other	$850	$850	$850	$850	$850	$10,200
Total Cash from Operations	$31,820	$37,850	$50,060	$59,670	$31,820	$419,170
New Investment						$0
New debt						$0
Sale of fixed assets						$0
TOTAL CASH INFLOWS	$31,820	$37,850	$50,060	$59,670	$31,820	$419,170
CASH DISBURSEMENTS						
VARIABLE						
Production costs	$24,325		$10,575	$24,675		$114,750
Licensing fees					$17,920	$32,480
Commissions			$5,590			$21,952
Contract labor	$370	$370	$740	$280	$370	$4,150
Freight	$740	$740	$1,480	$560	$740	$8,300
Total cost of goods sold	$25,435	$1,110	$18,385	$25,515	$19,030	$181,632
Travel	$200	$500	$500	$500	$300	$4,400
Meals & entertainment	$150	$400	$400	$400	$400	$3,500
TOTAL VARIABLE	$25,785	$2,010	$19,285	$26,415	$19,730	$189,532
FIXED						
Salaries	$8,000	$8,000	$12,000	$8,000	$8,000	$98,500
Payroll taxes	$800	$800	$1,200	$800	$800	$9,850
Benefits	$2,000	$2,000	$3,000	$2,000	$2,000	$24,625
Rent	$1,000	$1,000	$1,000	$1,000	$1,000	$12,000
Utilities	$200	$250	$250	$300	$300	$3,100
Insurance						$1,800
Marketing & advertising	$5,550	$5,550	$11,100	$4,200	$5,550	$62,250
Professional fees		$600			$600	$2,400
Telephone	$400	$400	$800	$800	$700	$7,100
Equipment leases	$300	$300	$300	$300	$300	$3,600
Repairs & maintenance	$100	$100	$100	$100	$100	$1,200
Miscellaneous	$100	$100	$100	$100	$100	$1,200
TOTAL FIXED	$18,450	$19,100	$29,850	$17,600	$19,450	$227,625
Principal & Interest: Loan 1		$450			$450	$1,800
Principal & Interest: Loan 2	$450	$450	$450	$450	$450	$5,400
Other (describe)						
TOTAL LOANS & OTHER	$450	$900	$450	$450	$900	$7,200
TOTAL CASH DISBURSEMENTS	$44,685	$22,010	$49,585	$44,465	$40,080	$424,357
CASH FLOW	($12,865)	$15,840	$475	$15,205	($8,260)	($5,187)
CUMULATIVE CASH FLOW	($28,447)	($12,607)	($12,132)	$3,073	($5,187)	
OPERATING CASH FLOW	($12,415)	$16,740	$925	$15,655	($7,360)	$2,013
STARTING CASH	($7,082)	($19,947)	($4,107)	($3,632)	$11,573	$8,500
+CASH INFLOWS	$31,820	$37,850	$50,060	$59,670	$31,820	$419,170
- CASH DISBURSEMENTS	$44,685	$22,010	$49,585	$44,465	$40,080	$424,357
ENDING CASH POSITION	($19,947)	($4,107)	($3,632)	$11,573	$3,313	$3,313

The cash-flow projection does more. Supposing there are no surprises in store, what else does it tell us? In the preceding example, **Effect of slow sales on cash flow**, it shows that no added cash will be needed to stay solvent, provided we stick to it. If sales differ from projections, the cash flow projection helps us understand the impact.

Suppose sales slump $50,000 in the first six months. What happens? The business would survive, but management would face substantial problems in August. Thanks to your managing by the numbers, you'd be able to arrange financing well in advance. This is a rough way to play "what if?" that serves very well if you have computerized a spreadsheet. Techniques like "Degree of Operating Leverage" (See Ch 10, "Strategic Analysis") are another approach to determining in advance what fluctuations in sales might do to your business.

The cash flow you've prepared will be used in Chs 7 and 8 ("Establishing Budgets," "Variance Analysis") as a key operating control.

The P&L and cash-flow projections together cover the dynamic aspects of running your business and provide the most effective standards against which to measure actual performance, since they reflect your business goals.

Chapter 5
The Balance Sheet

The balance sheet displays what you own (the assets of the business) and what you owe (liabilities). The difference between the assets and liabilities is the net worth of the business. As with the P&L and cash flow, you need some familiarity with the balance sheet to benefit fully from managing by the numbers. The format of the balance sheet is rigid: both assets and liabilities are listed in order of decreasing liquidity. The list of assets starts with cash and ends with the least liquid fixed assets; liabilities start with those bills you must meet now and end with the most remote.

Running a business efficiently and profitably calls for attaining and maintaining a delicate balance between and among all the balance sheet items. In Ch10 this notion will receive considerable attention. For now, just note that you need enough cash to meet current obligations, but not too much. Cash is not a productive asset. You can actually reduce your profits by paying bills too soon. The ratios of Ch 9 will help you gauge the shape of your business, "shape" being the relative size and composition of assets, liabilities, and net worth. Some guidelines (especially useful for new businesses) can be gleaned from the usual trade and industry sources. Others come from your past financial statements.

Once again, trends reveal what your business is doing. Is net worth increasing, decreasing, or stable from one year to the next? Net worth is driven by net profit from the P&L. Are assets increasing or decreasing? How does the shape stack up against industry and historic standards? The heart of managing by the numbers is measuring performance against standards, and the balance sheet provides a wealth of information.

Get monthly balance sheets. With a computerized accounting system this is a trifling task, with a manual one-write accounting system it may take an hour or so. An annual balance sheet to please the IRS and your bank is of no use in running your business: you get too little information too late.

Balance Sheet Format

Name of Company _____

Date_____

ASSETS	LIABILITIES
Cash	Accounts payable
Accounts receivable	Current portion long-term debt
Inventory	Notes payable
Pre-paid expense	Accrued expenses
Other	Income taxes payable
TOTAL CURRENT ASSETS	Other current liabilities
	TOTAL CURRENT LIABILITIES
Fixtures	Notes payable (long-term)
Vehicles	Bank loans payable
Equipment	Deferred taxes
Leasehold improvements	Other loans payable
Building	Other long term liabilities
Land	TOTAL LONG-TERM LIABILITIES
Accumulated depreciation	
Intangibles	RETAINED EARNINGS
Other fixed assets	INVESTED CAPITAL
TOTAL FIXED ASSETS	NET WORTH
TOTAL ASSETS	TOTAL LIABILITIES AND NET WORTH

Balance sheet example

These figures in the following balance sheet are used for example only. The explanation of the items and the format are generic. and may help you understand your own balance sheets better.

Cash, on hand or in checking or savings accounts.

Accounts receivable. Money owed to the company by its customers. In this example, look at cash flow worksheet 1 in Ch 4. The receivables which turn to cash in February were generated in January, so accounts receivable in January will be approximately equal to cash from receivables in February. The correlation is not exact. There will always be some slippage from one period to the next, and forecasts (as often noted) are never 100% accurate.

Inventory. Carried at cost. Inventory accounts are more complex for manufacturers and retailers. Your accountant will advise you on how to value inventory, as it has substantial tax implications.

Pre-paid expense. Deposits, advances on salaries, etc.

Other. Any other current asset. This might be office supplies, for example.

ASSETS

Cash	$8,500
Accounts receivable	$33,000
Inventory	$30,000
Prepaid expenses	$2,000
Other	$1,000
TOTAL CURRENT ASSETS	$74,500
Fixtures	$2,500
Vehicles	$4,000
Equipment	$18,000
Leasehold improvements	$10,000
Buildings	$0
Land	$0
Accumulated depreciation	($12,000)
Intangibles	$0
Other fixed assets	$0
TOTAL FIXED ASSETS	$22,500
TOTAL ASSETS	$97,000

LIABILITIES

Accounts payable	$15,000
Current portion of long-term debt	$5,400
Notes payable	$2,000
Accrued expenses	$2,400
Income taxes payable	$0
Other current liabilities	$1,200
TOTAL CURRENT LIABILITIES	$26,000
Notes payable (long-term)	$0
Bank loans payable	$8,000
Deferred taxes	$0
Other loans payable	$12,000
Other long-term liabilities	$0
TOTAL LONG-TERM LIABILITIES	$20,000
TOTAL LIABILITIES	$46,000
Retained earnings	$25,000
Invested capital	$26,000
Other	
TOTAL NET WORTH	$51,000
TOTAL LIABILITIES & NET WORTH	$97,000

Accumulated depreciation. Fixed assets are "written off" over their anticipated life according to methods set by the Internal Revenue Service. On the P&L in Ch 2, see the line "amortization and depreciation." This is a non-cash expense which reduces taxable income; the underlying concept is that you use up depreciable assets at a predictable pace and should be able to expense it over that period. The $300/month increases the depreciation on the balance sheet by a similar amount. Let your accountant worry about this. It doesn't affect operations.

Intangibles include goodwill, value of copyrights and patents, and so on. The depreciation of an intangible is called amortization. Leave these values to your CPA.

Accounts payable. What you owe other businesses except banks and a few others, which are broken out separately.

Current portion of long-term debt. Normally, the amount you are obligated to pay this year (the next 12 months) to your bank. $450 x 12 = $5,400. See the cash flow.

Notes payable. Includes interest. Usually short-term.

Accrued expenses. Expenses incurred but not yet paid. Salaries, etc.

Other. In this case, interest payable on office loan.

Bank loans payable. Bank debt minus the current portion of long-term debt. This figure has been rounded off for clarity.

Other loans payable. Officer loan. This could also have appeared on the line "other." If the loan is subordinated to all other company obligations, it would have appeared on the line "subordinated debt."

Retained earnings are equal to total assets minus total liabilities plus invested capital plus other. This is arguably the most obscure portion of the balance sheet, but remember the basic balance-sheet equation:

$$\text{Assets} = \text{liabilities plus net worth}$$

This equation is always true. Retained earnings will fluctuate month by month. The trend and pattern is important; the small fluctuations are not.

Net worth. Book value of the business, not to be confused with market value, which is the amount an informed buyer would pay an informed seller in an arms-length transaction. Since

$$\text{Assets minus liabilities} = \text{net worth}$$

you aim to increase assets and decrease liabilities to improve net worth. You will have a "negative net worth" if your liabilities exceed your assets, a condition bankers abhor. In most cases, bankers cannot lend money to a business with a negative net worth.

Projected balance sheets aren't often used in small businesses, though occasionally an investor or banker will request one. If that happens, have your accountant prepare it (plus whatever other schedules are needed), because it gets tricky. The changes in the various balance-sheet entries are driven by both the P&L and the cash flow: if sales go up, for example, your accounts receivable and accounts payable will usually rise as well. So will inventories and the various loans payable. Cash is forecast by the cash flow, but how you will actually employ that cash requires further thought.

If this sounds complex, it is. Yet a projected balance sheet provides useful guidelines. Sit down with your accountant and go through an exercise in which you tie your goals (expressed in your projected P&L and cash flow) to an idealized balance sheet, then work backwards to ascertain what steps are going to get you there.

The short-term use of your monthly balance sheet is simple: Observe the changes over time. Any radical departure should be traced back to its cause. If you have a set of balance-sheet-related goals, track them too. (See Ch 9 for key ratios.) These include improving the cash position, turning receivables faster, and controlling inventories. Such goals are important because accounts receivable and inventories are the dominant asset accounts. Keeping payables under control is another operating goal, a key indicator worth tracking.

Balance sheet comparison form

Short-term fluctuations in net worth are not of great concern, but the trend is. By using a form such as the balance sheet comparison form shown below to ride herd on the balance sheet, or by graphing monthly changes, you will discover new and interesting patterns in your business, which will lead to improved forecasts and performance.

The three main financial statements are interrelated. Several examples have been noted—the progression from the P&L to the cash flow to the balance sheet. As you pay down an equipment loan, for example, several things happen:

P&L: You incur interest expense and a non-cash depreciation expense.

Cash flow: Principal and interest disbursements are recorded.

BS: Current portion of long-term debt is lowered: accumulated depreciation increases.

Changes ripple through the P&L, cash flow, and balance sheet in more subtle ways. The interrelations are established so a skilled accountant or auditor will pick up any fudged numbers. You don't have to be an accountant to use these statements, just versed enough to raise questions if the numbers don't add up or feel right. That ability comes from experience in looking at the numbers, comparing them to standards and looking for the discrepancies.

The next and final step is to test your forecasts against historical and trade or industry figures. The choice is influenced by your experience and your plans, as well as the stage of your business.

Ed Kearney, a management consultant and industrial engineer from Portland, Maine, makes a good and pithy argument against relying on Robert Morris Associates or other broadly generated figures: He says they can only tell you you don't have cancer. Since they are based on a large number of business of all sizes and ages, they establish general parameters. True, bankers and other investors use them. But for many small businesses, the RMA figures are not only inappropriate but seriously misleading.

ASSETS	Q1	Q2	Q3	Q4
Cash	$8,500	$8,000		
Accounts receivable	$33,000	$22,400		
Inventory	$30,000	$44,000		
Prepaid expenses	$2,000	$600		
Other	$1,000	$200		
TOTAL CURRENT ASSETS:	$74,500	$75,200		
Fixtures	$2,500	$2,500		
Vehicles	$4,000	$4,000		
Equipment	$18,000	$18,000		
Leasehold improvements	$10,000	$10,000		
Buildings	$0	$0		
Land	$0	$0		
Accumulated depreciation	($12,000)	($12,300)		
Intangibles	$0	$0		
Other fixed assets	$0	$0		
TOTAL FIXED ASSETS	$22,500	$22,200		
TOTAL ASSETS	$97,000	$97,400		
LIABILITIES				
Accounts payable	$15,000	$12,000		
Current portion of long term debt	$5,400	$4,950		
Notes payable	$2,000	$2,000		
Accrued expenses	$2,400	$0		
Income taxes payable	$0	$0		
Other current liabilities	$1,200	$1,200		
TOTAL CURRENT LIABILITIES	$26,000	$20,150		
Notes payable (long-term)	$0	$0		
Bank loans payable	$8,000	$8,000		
Deferred taxes	$0	$0		
Other loans payable	$12,000	$12,000		
Other long term liabilities	$0	$0		
TOTAL LONG TERM LIABILITIES	$20,000	$20,000		
TOTAL LIABILITIES	$46,000	$40,150		
Retained earnings	$25,000	$31,250		
Invested capital	$26,000	$26,000		
Other	$0	$0		
TOTAL NET WORTH	$51,000	$57,250		
TOTAL LIABILITIES & NET WORTH	$97,000	$97,400		

For other businesses, RMA and similar compilations of data can be more useful. Make sure to check out your industry or trade associations, because trade and industry standards, if they fit your business, are invaluable. The closer the fit, the better. Ask yourself:

• Are the businesses similar to yours, apples to apples? A drugstore is not a gift store. This is the biggest weakness of aggregated statistics. While all businesses in retailing share certain problems, a jeweler, a grocer and a drugstore have dissimilar sales, receivables, inventory and capital pictures. Finding a close fit from any but precise trade sources is almost always frustrating. Timing warps this even more. RMA figures are always a year or more old. The patterns are relatively stable, however, so they form a general guide.

• Same size? A $1 million business has a different shape from a $100,000 business.

• Same kind of markets? If you sell primarily to institutions rather than individuals, your financials will differ from a business selling the same products to individual customers.

• "All things being equal"? Historical financial figures from a boom period have little relevance in a bust period. Regional and local economic conditions have a profound impact on your business, for good or bad.

The very best standards come from a combination of sources. Your historical experience, business plan, trade figures and one or more of the aggregated sources all work together. The checks and balances are ways to make sure your forecasts are well-grounded.

Summary

Your forecasts, based on available information and your goals for the next year, provide a balanced set of company-wide standards to shoot for. As the year wears on, new forecasts, based on changes in circumstances, may be appropriate. Just make sure not to change goals too often. Revising forecasts every six months pays off. Revisions on a monthly basis usually don't.

Compare your forecasts against historical and trade or industry data to ensure a fairly safe set of standards and an adequate level of thoroughness. Experience builds fast. Leave a major expense out of your P&L once and you'll not do so again.

Chapter 6
Break-even Analysis

Break-even analysis comes in two flavors: P&L or cash flow. Either one will help in a large number of decisions: Should you buy or lease that piece of equipment? Should you hire that salesperson now or later? Will you be able to produce the required sales volume? The uses are limited only by your willingness to use break-even analysis as a guide to decision-making.

Break-even analysis is no silver bullet. Very few small business owners use it. The basic idea that break-even analysis is built on is that covering the nut, those fixed monthly expenses that have to be met no matter what level of sales you achieve, together with variable expenses, establishes a base sales level at which you neither make or lose money. Schematically, it develops like this: Costs in dollars are plotted on the vertical axis, sales in dollars on the horizontal axis. The diagonal line is where sales exactly equal costs.

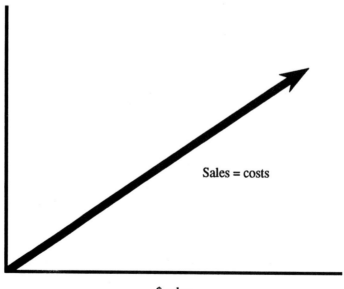

Fixed costs are the same no matter what the sales level is, so they are represented by a horizontal line parallel to the sales axis. The point where the fixed cost and cost = sales lines intersect would be the break-even point for a business with no variable costs. I've never seen such a business, but I suppose one might exist. Perhaps on another planet, or in another economy.

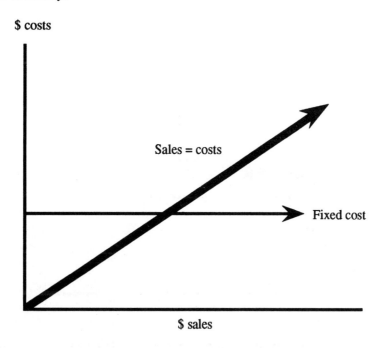

Variable costs by definition don't begin until a sale is made. The sum of fixed and variable costs equals the total cost, shown schematically by the heavy diagonal arrow.

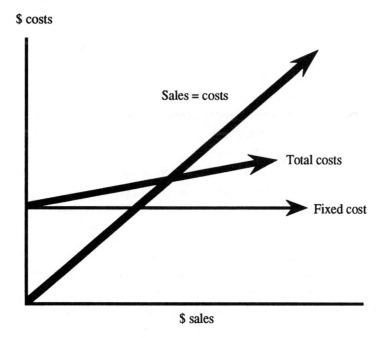

If fixed costs were $0, the diagonal would begin at the intersection of the cost and sales axes. Since there are fixed costs in most businesses, we simply start adding he variable costs at the intersection of $0 sales and whatever the fixed costs happen to be. This generates the total cost line.

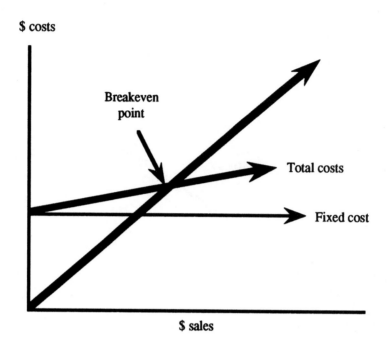

The break-even point is the intersection of the total cost and cost = sales lines. At this point, sales will generate exactly the revenue needed to cover all costs.

This can be expressed mathematically. The formulas are:

Cash breakeven = fixed costs + [1 − (variable costs + sales)]

P&L breakeven = fixed expenses + [1 − (variable expenses + sales)]

The beauty of break-even analysis is that given the basic formulas you can express your business's break-even point in terms of units sold, numbers of customers or similar familiar quantities. One example I'll never forget is a small restaurant whose owner figured his break-even as bowls of soup sold per day. He discovered that his restaurant couldn't serve enough customers during peak periods to come close to break-even, so he changed his marketing strategy to a highly profitable luncheon take-out and delivery operation. Managing by the numbers sometimes leads to unexpected results.

Some useful conversions:

Annual b/e + 12 = monthly sales needed = monthly b/e
Monthly b/e + 4.3 = weekly sales needed = weekly b/e
Weekly b/e + work days = daily sales needed = daily b/e
Daily b/e + hours worked = average hourly sales needed = average b/e
Average b/e + average price = units that have to be sold per hour

> Monthly b/e ÷ average price = units that have to be sold per month
> Daily b/e ÷ average price = units that have to be sold per day ("bowls of soup")

Break-even analysis proceeds simply. Fixed expenses or costs are (relatively) independent of sales. Keep in mind that they are fixed only within limits, because if sales grow dramatically, the fixed costs will be forced to change too, albeit erratically, in a discontinuous step function rather than a smooth, controllable curve. If you move to larger quarters, bang! rent moves from $1,000/month to $5,000/month. Personnel costs hurtle upward. New equipment and more vehicles are necessary.

But with that warning in mind, many expenses can be treated as if they were fixed. Most are clear: rent, loan payments, payroll. A few seem a bit murky: Is telephone fixed or variable? To be conservative, allocate any questionable item to fixed. A more aggressive approach is to split the cost, assigning a portion to each. Happily these items in the middle are not only few in number, they also tend to be small in amount.

Should you use a cash flow or P&L break-even analysis? I prefer to use the P&L break-even analysis and add profit goals to the fixed expenses. If a business were in a start-up or transitional mode, it should use a cash flow break-even analysis. Tom Weber says you should always look at the cash flow break-even first, paying special attention to operating needs. The break-even helps answer the questions: Is it necessary? Can we do without it? Why do we need it? How can we pay for it? These questions come up whenever a capital investment is contemplated.

Start-ups and businesses in transition: Use cash flow break-even analysis

Ongoing businesses: Use P&L break-even analysis

Fast-growth businesses: Use both cash flow and P&L break-even analysis. You need all the help you can get. Break-even analysis is a fine aid to growth and survival.

As an example, look at the one-year P&L projection in Ch 3. Follow the same process for your business if you will be using a P&L break-even analysis.

1. Allocate expenses to fixed or variable. All of the cost of goods sold are variable. The only other apparent variable expense is marketing and advertising. For reasons mentioned earlier, we arbitrarily assigned this to fixed. You might choose to assign this 50/50 or some other way. Managing by the numbers doesn't dictate this choice. Experience does.

Using historical patterns rather than your projected or forecast figures is dangerous unless you feel confident that next year will be very much the same as last. Using forecasts links your plans and goals more closely to operating realities and affords better standards.

2. Add your profit goals to fixed expenses. This again is optional. You are not in business to fall short of your goals. Treat profit as a fixed expense.

3. Add the totals and do the arithmetic.

Fixed expenses = $252,000 + $42,000 = $294,000

Variable expenses = $180,000

Sales = $475,000

(P&L) b/e = fixed expenses ÷ [1 - (variable expenses ÷ sales)]

$$= \$294,000 \div [1 - (\$180,000 \div \$475,000)]$$

$$= \$290,000 \div (1 - 0.38)$$

4. Profit b/e = $294,000 ÷ 0.62 = $474,000

If we didn't add back pre-tax profit (to eliminate the impact of taxes):

5. (P&L) break-even analysis = $252,000 ÷ 0.62 = $406,000

Compare 5 based on a P&L break-even to the cash flow break-even derived from the preliminary cash flow in Ch 4:

Fixed costs + other costs + marketing and advertising costs = $165,300 + $7,200 + $70,000 = $243,000

Fixed costs (disbursements) = $243,000

Variable costs (disbursements) = $206,000

Cash inflows from sales = $469,000

(Cash) b/e = $243,000 ÷ [1-($206,000 ÷ $469,000)]

= $243,000 ÷ (1 - 0.44)

= $434,000 ÷ 0.56

The difference is important. Cash needs for break-even exceed the P&L break-even and is about midway between it and (4), which included profit. The conclusion? The cash-flow-based break-even is more conservative than the P&L-based break-even. If your business is on the edge, use the cash-flow version to monitor progress. Survival is your primary goal. If undergoing rapid change, use both methods.

How would these figures be used? Here are a couple of ways.

1. Number of units per year. Assume the average price per unit is $10. You have to sell nearly 50,000 units to make profit goals, 44,000 to break even on cash. What if you raised prices to an average $12/unit? Your cash break-even drops to 36,000 units, while your profit break-even drops to 40,000 units. Now this may or may not be achievable. Pricing points are sensitive issues and a rise in price might seriously hurt sales. No business decision is made in a vacuum, but break-even analysis gives you some roughly accurate numbers to help inform your pricing decisions.

Note that these are only roughly accurate. Lower unit sales translate into somewhat lowered production costs (COGS), which would make break-even more attainable. Yet again: if you err, let it be in the direction of caution. The sense of accuracy gained by re-juggling the P&L and cash flow isn't worth the effort. Managing by the numbers doesn't require such fine-tuning and indeed is somewhat scornful of the effort. Better have a simple tool you use than a complicated one you let rust in its box.

2. Profit break-even of 50,000 units equals approximately 1,000 units a week or 4,000 units per month. How will these sales be gained? Or given the patterns of historical sales, should you look to longer periods as an ongoing measure? A rolling three-month average? Perhaps. Sales are made one by one. If the average sale is ten units, then you need 5,000 sales, or 400 per month. These ruminations help set strategies and monitor progress. As you'll see in Ch 12, these figures will be worked backwards up the sales funnel and expressed in such terms as numbers of calls, prospecting and other, letters and marketing concentrations. Never forget that sales drive everything. The numbers are useful in getting sales and in improving the selling process.

3. What happens if you add a salesperson at a cost of $30,000 plus expenses of $6,000 and a 6% sales commission? How many sales dollars must she generate to pay for herself—let alone generate a profit—and is it likely that she'll make those sales?

The math is simple:

$$\text{Fixed cost} \div [1 - (0.44 + 0.06)] = \$36{,}000 \div 0.5 = \$72{,}000$$

This is an approximation, but close enough to help you make a rational decision. Are sales of $72,000 achievable? Perhaps. It depends on the context. It represents 7,200 units for a year, or an average of 600 units per month. For a beginner, is this realistic? The answer depends on how other salespeople have initially performed, how strong the territory and competition and the economy are, and the experience and training of the individual herself.

What kind of business are you in?

An important line of thought proceeds from looking at the composition of your costs:

1. Service industries typically have low fixed costs and medium variable costs, resulting in a low break-even point. Profits go up with sales once the break-even is reached.

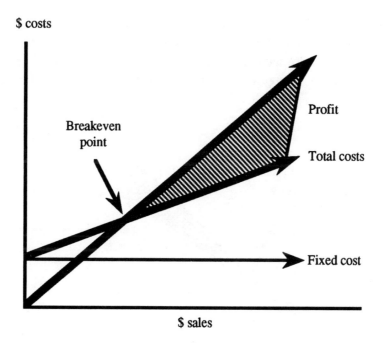

2. Manufacturers usually have high fixed costs and low variable costs. Once break-even is finally reached, small sales increases lead to large profit increases:

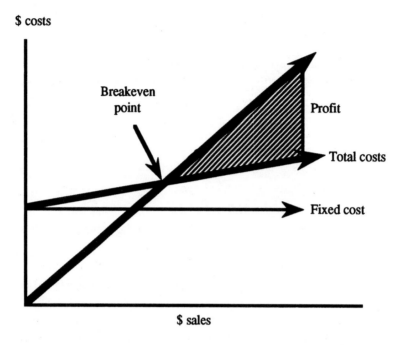

3. Construction firms have low fixed costs and high variable costs, leading to a high break-even point. Large sales increases lead to relatively little increases in profit, which can cause cash problems, though if the numbers are large enough, profits can be immense.

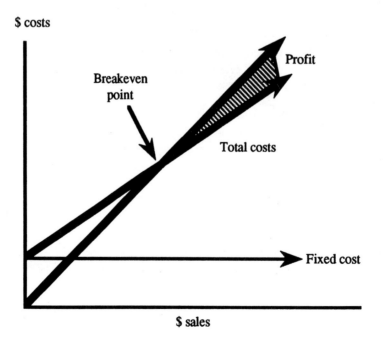

You should know the cost pattern of your business. If you are heavy with fixed costs, first prune those costs as much as possible and then drive the revenues up. If fixed costs are relatively low but variable costs are high, look for economies on the variable costs first, then drive revenues up. This assumes, of course, that these changes are made in the context of your more general business plans. Recognition of your cost patterns can help you decide whether cost cutting or pushing for higher revenues would be more appropriate for your firm. Usually it will turn out to be a combination of efforts, on both the cost reduction and revenue improvement sides, but you benefit from knowing which strategy will yield the best returns.

Degree of operating leverage

Degree of operating leverage (DOL) is a tool closely related to break-even analysis. DOL utilizes variable costs, accounts receivable, accounts payable, inventory and cash to determine what sales increase is needed to generate a dollar of cash.

Many of us, when confronted by a cash squeeze, think we can quickly generate sales to pull in enough cash, fast enough, to relieve the pressure. While this may work (and in some ways must be the long-term solution), two forces make it unlikely. The first is the business truism that sales never turn to cash as fast as you hope they will. It takes time for your customers to pay, especially if you offer credit or extended payment terms. It takes time to process the invoice, time for the Post Office to move an envelope across town, time to cut the check once the customer receives the invoice, time for the check to be mailed back to your office.

The other force is DOL. As sales rise, so do a host of related costs. You need more inventory, perhaps more variable labor to push orders through. The net effect: you will raise less money, and over a longer time, than you plan.

The DOL formula:

$$DOL = S + [S - V - (CE + A/R + I - A/P)(1 - T)]$$

where
S = Total sales
V = Variable costs
CF = Cash and equivalent
A/R = Accounts receivable
I = Inventory
A/P = Accounts payable
T = Income tax rate (in the example, 10%)

This example uses figures from the balance sheet in Ch 5 and the cash flow in Ch 4.

DOL = $469,000 + [$469,000 - $206,000 -

$$- (\$8,000 + \$33,000 + \$30,000 - \$15,000)(1 - 0.10)]$$

$$= \$469,000 + \$186,000 = \$2.52$$

In other words, a sales increase of $2.52 results in a cash increase of $1.00. Just how long it will take to generate this hypothetical dollar is another matter. An average retail store needs a sales increase of over $5 to generate a single solitary $1 of cash. Your business's DOL will naturally depend on your business's distribution of costs and balance sheet.

Note that high cash, accounts receivable and inventory figures will increase your DOL, while higher accounts payable will tend to decrease your DOL. This means that if you can safely run your business with lean cash and inventory, and keep accounts receivable low by diligent collection efforts, your sales will turn to cash more rapidly. Reducing accounts payable, on the other hand, may be a poor strategy. Pay on time and take discounts—but don't pre-pay.

The implications of DOL vary from one business to another, but the underlying principle is the same. A dollar increase in sales is usually a slower route to generating cash than careful management of accounts receivable and accounts payable.

Conclusions

Break-even analysis is a simple, powerful aid to decision making. When contemplating adding an expense or tinkering with prices, ask yourself what impact it will have on the break-even point. One checkpoint among many others, break-even analysis shouldn't be used in isolation.

DOL is less often used, but it illustrates the effect your variable costs and some balance-sheet items have on your ability to generate cash internally. You may find the numbers for your business are surprising and decide to alter your current asset management policies and stretch payables as a preferred means of generating cash in a hurry.

Chapter 7
Establishing Budgets:
P&L and Cash Flow

Budgets are essential management tools. Businesses that run without budgets suffer chronic cash shortages, problems with vendors, don't thrive and sooner or later vanish. The ideas behind a business may be terrific, the energy and commitment total, the customers supportive, but the discipline and control of establishing and then following a budget is needed to hold all the pieces together.

The trick has always been to establish a budget that reflects your business and its resources, opportunities, problems and plans.

Managing by the numbers and budgets are inseparable. The P&L and cash-flow projections established earlier are the core of your budgets. For many small businesses the projections provide plenty of detail to manage the business well. Other businesses will want additional budgets, for example, a separate marketing and advertising budget. Another useful budget is the capital budget for major purchases such as plant and equipment. Such capital assets are usually well-thought out purchases, though not always. Some of us get carried away by the excitement of new equipment. If you ever visit my business, ask to have a tour of my personal computer museum.

Budgets are established for two reasons. First, you want to make sure that money is available when it is needed and that all expenditures further your company's business goals. Second, money has a penchant for dribbling away. A few dollars here and there can add up surprisingly fast and leave no traces. If you make all disbursements by check, you at least have a record of where the money goes. If you make many checks out to cash, your records won't help you at all and the IRS will assess personal income taxes on you, as their reasonable presumption will be that these are personal expenses. Leasing a copying machine may only cost $50/month. That's $600 a year, straight to the fixed-cost column. If the expense was not budgeted because of the dubious rationale of "it's only $50/month" chances are it is not a justified expense.

Budgets are established in three ways: top down (imposed by management as a way to reach profit goals), bottom up, or collaboratively. Each method has strong advocates. The larger the business, the more likely it is that the budget will be dictated from above, negotiated with the managers involved and adhered to rigidly. That's why large businesses make large profits. They carefully craft their budgets and stick to them. Performance and salary reviews focus on how well or poorly managers hew to their assigned budgets.

Very small businesses often have no budgets at all, or have such fluid budgets that any excuse to violate them will be accepted. Such budgets as they do have tend to be a hodgepodge of ideas from all corners.

The compromise position, the collaborative budget, includes the managers in the budgeting process from the start. If you have only a few employees, this is far and away the best method to follow. You explain your goals; your employees then help figure out how to attain them. Your employees will know the goals, see how the budget helps attain the goals, and will be less apt to resist budgetary constraints since they understand the reasoning.

A cash-flow budget is always best for start-ups, businesses in transition, and fast-growth businesses concerned with liquidity. Ongoing businesses prefer the P&L budget, as their interest is focused on profitability. In an ideal world you'd use both budgets on a monthly, rolling quarterly and year-to-date basis. (These methods are more fully explained in Ch 8, "Variance Analysis.")

The process is the same for each:

1. Establish the one-year forecast or pro forma.
2. Think through possible capital expenditures.
3. Examine financing needs and options.
4. Work capital expenditures and financing into the P&L and cash-flow projections.

Impact on Cash Flow Budget

To illustrate the process, look at **Cash-flow budget**. This is the budget for the next 12 months. The cash-flow changes involved (and their rationale) are as follows:

New investment of $40,000 will beef up the balance sheet, provide basis for further borrowing in anticipation of a substantial acquisition in June. The acquisition may be larger inventories, equipment or whatever. Any major disbursement must be budgeted and steps taken ahead of time to ensure funding. Assume that you plan to acquire a small competitor. You don't anticipate generating revenues for at least 18 months after signing the deal, so there will be no immediate impact on the cash flow or P&L except as noted here and below.

New debt in June: $60,000. This is the second part of financing the acquisition. A six-month lead time is not unusual. Budgets are concerned (as is the cash flow) with amounts and timing.

Other. The acquisition occurs—or is expected to—in June.

Other. Repayment begins. These payments include principal and interest. A flat-rate payment of this kind reduces interest paid, and, if cash flow permits, is in your favor. The terms are for a three-year payback, quarterly payments, last payment a balloon. Don't worry about how this is structured. Your banker can explain. The underlying idea: fit the term of the payback to the useful life of the purchased asset.

Cash flow budget

(Memo sales figures)							
$28,000	$47,000	$28,000	$37,000	$37,000	$47,000	$28,000	$28,000
	Jan	**Feb**	**Mar**	**Apr**	**May**	**Jun**	**Jul**
CASH INFLOWS							
Cash sales	$15,510	$9,240	$12,210	$12,210	$15,510	$9,240	$9,240
Cash from receivables	$18,760	$31,490	$18,760	$24,790	$24,790	$31,490	$18,760
Other	$850	$850	$850	$850	$850	$850	$850
Total cash from operations	$35,120	$41,580	$31,820	$37,850	$41,150	$41,580	$28,850
New investment			$40,000				
New debt						$60,000	
Sale of fixed assets							
TOTAL CASH IN	$35,120	$41,580	$71,820	$37,850	$41,150	$101,580	$28,850
CASH DISBURSEMENTS							
VARIABLE DISBURSEMENTS							
Production costs	$9,075	$21,175			$9,075	$21,175		$10,425
Licensing fees							$17,920	
Commissions	$5,294			$6,511			$7,235
Contract labor	$470	$280	$370	$370	$470	$280	$280
Freight	$940	$560	$740	$740	$940	$560	$560
Total COGS:	$15,779	$22,015	$1,110	$16,696	$22,585	$18,760	$18,500
Travel	$300	$300	$200	$200	$200	$1,000	$200
Meals & entertainment	$200	$200	$150	$150	$150	$750	$150
TOTAL VARIABLE	$16,279	$22,515	$1,460	$17,046	$22,935	$20,510	$18,850
FIXED DISBURSEMENTS							
Salaries	$7,000	$7,000	$10,500	$7,000	$7,000	$8,000	$8,000
Payroll taxes	$700	$700	$1,050	$700	$700	$800	$800
Benefits	$1,750	$1,750	$2,625	$1,750	$1,750	$2,000	$2,000
Rent	$1,000	$1,000	$1,000	$1,000	$1,000	$1,000	$1,000
Utilities	$300	$300	$300	$250	$250	$200	$200
Insurance	$900					$900	
Marketing & advertising	$7,050	$4,200	$5,550	$5,550	$7,050	$4,200	$4,200
Professional fees			$600			$600	
Telephone	$600	$600	$600	$600	$600	$600	$400
Equipment leases	$300	$300	$300	$300	$300	$300	$300
Repairs & maintenance	$100	$100	$100	$100	$100	$100	$100
Miscellaneous	$100	$100	$100	$100	$100	$100	$100
TOTAL FIXED	$19,800	$16,050	$22,725	$17,350	$18,850	$18,800	$17,100
P & I: Loan 1			$450			$450	
P & I: Loan 2	$450	$450	$450	$450	$450	$450	$450
Other: (describe)						$80,000	
Other: (describe)							
TOTAL OTHER	$450	$450	$900	$450	$450	$80,900	$450
TOTAL DISBURSEMENTS	$36,529	$39,015	$25,085	$34,846	$42,235	$120,210	$36,400
CASH FLOW	($1,409)	$2,565	$46,735	$3,004	($1,085)	($18,630)	($7,550)
CUM. CASH FLOW	($1,409)	$1,156	$47,891	$50,894	$49,809	$31,179	$23,630
OPERATING CASH FLOW	($959)	$3,015	$7,635	$3,454	($635)	$2,270	($7,100)
STARTING CASH	$8,500	$7,091	$9,656	$56,391	$59,394	$58,309	$39,679
+CASH INFLOWS	$35,120	$41,580	$71,820	$37,850	$41,150	$101,580	$28,850
- CASH DISBURSEMENTS	$36,529	$39,015	$25,085	$34,846	$42,235	$120,210	$36,400
ENDING CASH POSITION	$7,091	$9,656	$56,391	$59,394	$58,309	$39,679	$32,130

Cash flow budget (cont.)

	Aug	Sep	Oct	Nov	Dec	TOTALS
(Memo sales figures)						TOTALS
$28,000	$37,000	$37,000	$74,000	$28,000	$37,000	$493,000
CASH INFLOWS						
Cash sales	$12,210	$12,210	$24,420	$9,240	$12,210	$153,450
Cash from receivables	$18,760	$24,790	$24,790	$49,580	$18,760	$305,520
Other	$850	$850	$850	$850	$850	$10,200
Total cash from operations	$31,820	$37,850	$50,060	$59,670	$31,820	$469,170
New investment						$40,000
New debt						$60,000
Sale of fixed assets						$0
TOTAL CASH IN	$31,820	$37,850	$50,060	$59,670	$31,820	$569,170
CASH DISBURSEMENTS						
VARIABLE DISBURSEMENTS						
Production costs	$24,325		$10,575	$24,675		$130,500
Licensing fees					$20,800	$38,720
Commissions			$5,911			$24,952
Contract labor	$370	$370	$740	$280	$370	$4,650
Freight	$740	$740	$1,480	$560	$740	$9,300
Total COGS:	$25,435	$1,110	$18,706	$25,515	$21,910	$208,122
Travel	$200	$500	$500	$500	$300	$4,400
Meals & entertainment	$150	$400	$400	$400	$400	$3,500
TOTAL VARIABLE	$25,785	$2,010	$19,606	$26,415	$22,610	$216,022
FIXED DISBURSEMENTS						
Salaries	$8,000	$8,000	$12,000	$8,000	$8,000	$98,500
Payroll taxes	$800	$800	$1,200	$800	$800	$9,850
Benefits	$2,000	$2,000	$3,000	$2,000	$2,000	$24,625
Rent	$1,000	$1,000	$1,000	$1,000	$1,000	$12,000
Utilities	$200	$250	$250	$300	$300	$3,100
Insurance						$1,800
Marketing & advertising	$5,550	$5,550	$11,100	$4,200	$5,550	$69,750
Professional fees		$600			$600	$2,400
Telephone	$400	$400	$800	$800	$700	$7,100
Equipment leases	$300	$300	$300	$300	$300	$3,600
Repairs & maintenance	$100	$100	$100	$100	$100	$1,200
Miscellaneous	$100	$100	$100	$100	$100	$1,200
TOTAL FIXED	$18,450	$19,100	$29,850	$17,600	$19,450	$235,125
P & I: Loan 1		$450			$450	$1,800
P & I: Loan 2	$450	$450	$450	$450	$450	$5,400
Other: (describe)						
Other: (describe)		$5,000			$5,000	
TOTAL OTHER	$450	$5,900	$450	$450	$5,900	$97,200
TOTAL DISBURSEMENTS	$44,685	$27,010	$49,906	$44,465	$47,960	$548,347
CASH FLOW	($12,865)	$10,840	$154	$15,205	($16,140)	$20,823
CUM. CASH FLOW	$10,765	$21,605	$21,758	$36,963	$20,823	
OPERATING CASH FLOW	($12,415)	$16,740	$604	$15,655	($10,240)	$18,023
STARTING CASH	$32,130	$19,265	$30,105	$30,258	$45,463	$8,500
+CASH INFLOWS	$31,820	$37,850	$50,060	$59,670	$31,820	$569,170
- CASH DISBURSEMENTS	$44,685	$27,010	$49,906	$44,465	$47,960	$548,347
ENDING CASH POSITION	$19,265	$30,105	$30,258	$45,463	$29,323	$29,323

Impact on P&L Budget

The impact of these changes on the cash flow are clear. This is how it affects the P&L. (See **P&L budget.**)

Interest, new loan. $1,800 in September, $1,700 in December. The capital payments don't appear; the purchase of the asset or acquisition and new debt and investment show up on the balance sheet, but not here on the P&L. This is an important difference to note between the P&L and cash-flow budgets: more detail of importance shows on the cash flow.

If you decide you need supplemental budgets, use the amount allotted in the preliminary steps of establishing your forecasts as a guideline. The P&L one-year forecast of Ch 3 provides the baseline for a marketing and advertising budget. The total amount allocated for the year, $69,750, has been spread over the year. The next step in such a supplemental budget is to identify where the money will be spent. Have a plan for all major expenditures (15% of sales is significant), rather than leaving it to the whim of the moment. Leave some slack in such a budget to accommodate unexpected events that arise or to take advantage of an opportunity.

The budget for marketing and advertising follows. Note that it is sketchy and includes both monthly and occasional expenses.

Presence advertising. $1,200/month. Includes all space ads.
Direct mail. $28,000/year. Includes art and copy, list rentals, postage, print.
Trade shows: $6,000/year.
Expertise: $1,000/month. All outside marketing help. Consultant, advertising agent.

The total of $69,750 is treated as if it were $60,000. In other words, sequester about 15% for those surprise expenses or opportunities. If you don't spend it all, it goes to profit. if you do spend it all, it goes (you hope!) to growth. The battle between current profit and future growth is ongoing. In successful businesses, future growth usually gets the nod.

The numbers come from experience, historical and industry figures and trends, goals and most importantly from long discussions with the marketing and sales managers, who in turn solicit ideas from their sources. For their own purposes, they might break the expenses down even further. They want to maximize the results of their expenditures too, as their bonus compensation depends on achieving profitable growth for the company as a whole.

Summary

Establishing budgets is difficult. Making budgets effective, putting them to work, is made easier by involving all key employees in the budgeting process from goal-setting through sales forecasts to the preliminary cash flow. Their insights strengthen the forecasts, add ideas you may have missed and give them a sense of ownership of the numbers. This is vital. Otherwise managing by the numbers can degenerate into an unproductive argument about numbers that are meaningless to your employees if not to you.

P&L budget

	Jan	Feb	Mar	Apr	May	Jun	Jul
SALES/REVENUE							
Products	$47,000	$28,000	$37,000	$37,000	$47,000	$28,000	$28,000
Other	$1,000	$1,000	$1,000	$1,000	$1,000	$1,000	$1,000
Returns & allowances	($150)	($150)	($150)	($150)	($150)	($150)	($150)
TOTAL REVENUES	$47,850	$28,850	$37,850	$37,850	$47,850	$28,850	$28,850
COST OF GOODS SOLD							
Production costs	$10,340	$6,160	$8,140	$8,140	$10,340	$6,160	$6,160
Licensing fees	$3,760	$2,240	$2,960	$2,960	$3,760	$2,240	$2,240
Commissions	$2,820	$1,680	$2,220	$2,220	$2,820	$1,680	$1,680
Contract labor	$470	$280	$370	$370	$470	$280	$280
Freight	$940	$560	$740	$740	$940	$560	$560
TOTAL COGS	$18,330	$10,920	$14,430	$14,430	$18,330	$10,920	$10,920
GROSS MARGIN	$29,520	$17,930	$23,420	$23,420	$29,520	$17,930	$17,930
OPERATING EXPENSES							
Salaries etc.	$10,000	$10,000	$10,000	$10,000	$10,000	$12,000	$12,000
Rent & utilities	$1,250	$1,250	$1,250	$1,250	$1,250	$1,250	$1,250
Insurance	$150	$150	$150	$150	$150	$150	$150
Marketing & advertising	$7,050	$4,200	$5,550	$5,550	$7,050	$4,200	$4,200
Travel	$300	$300	$200	$200	$200	$1,000	$200
Meals & entertainment	$200	$200	$150	$150	$150	$750	$150
Professional fees	$200	$200	$200	$200	$200	$200	$200
Telephone	$600	$600	$600	$600	$600	$400	$400
Equipment leases	$350	$350	$350	$350	$350	$350	$350
Repairs & maintenance	$100	$100	$100	$100	$100	$100	$100
Amort & depreciation	$300	$300	$300	$300	$300	$300	$300
Miscellaneous	$100	$100	$100	$100	$100	$100	$100
Interest expense	$300	$300	$300	$300	$300	$300	$300
NEW LOAN							
TOTAL OP. EXPENSES	$20,900	$18,050	$19,250	$19,250	$20,750	$21,100	$19,700
PRE-TAX PROFIT (LOSS)	$8,620	($120)	$4,170	$4,170	$8,770	($3,170)	($1,770)
Fed. taxes	$0	$0	$0	$0	$0	$0	$0
State taxes	$517	($7)	$250	$250	$526	($190)	($106)
CUM PROFIT (LOSS) PRE-TAX	$8,620	$8,500	$12,670	$16,840	$25,610	$22,440	$20,670
NET PROFIT (LOSS)	$8,103	($113)	$3,920	$3,920	$8,244	($2,980)	($1,664)

P&L budget (cont.)

	Aug	Sep	Oct	Nov	Dec	TOTALS	% of rev.
SALES/REVENUE							
Products	$37,000	$37,000	$74,000	$28,000	$37,000	$465,000	98%
Other	$1,000	$1,000	$1,000	$1,000	$1,000	$12,000	3%
Returns & allowances	($150)	($150)	($150)	($150)	($150)	($1,800)	-0.38%
TOTAL REVENUES	$37,850	$37,850	$74,850	$28,850	$37,850	$475,200	100%
COST OF GOODS SOLD							
Production costs	$8,140	$8,140	$16,280	$6,160	$8,140	$102,300	22%
Licensing fees	$2,960	$2,960	$5,920	$2,240	$2,960	$37,200	8%
Commissions	$2,220	$2,220	$4,440	$1,680	$2,220	$27,900	6%
Contract labor	$370	$370	$740	$280	$370	$4,650	1%
Freight	$740	$740	$1,480	$560	$740	$9,300	2%
TOTAL COGS	$14,430	$14,430	$28,860	$10,920	$14,430	$181,350	38%
GROSS MARGIN	$23,420	$23,420	$45,990	$17,930	$23,420	$293,850	62%
OPERATING EXPENSES							
Salaries etc.	$12,000	$12,000	$12,000	$12,000	$12,000	$134,000	28%
Rent & utilities	$1,250	$1,250	$1,250	$1,250	$1,250	$15,000	3%
Insurance	$150	$150	$150	$150	$150	$1,800	0.38%
Marketing & advertising	$5,550	$5,550	$11,100	$4,200	$5,550	$69,750	15%
Travel	$200	$500	$500	$500	$300	$4,400	1%
Meals & entertainment	$150	$400	$400	$400	$400	$3,500	1%
Professional fees	$200	$200	$200	$200	$200	$2,400	1%
Telephone	$400	$800	$800	$700	$600	$7,100	1%
Equipment leases	$350	$350	$350	$350	$350	$4,200	1%
Repairs & maintenance	$100	$100	$100	$100	$100	$1,200	0.25%
Amort & depreciation	$300	$300	$300	$300	$300	$3,600	1%
Miscellaneous	$100	$100	$100	$100	$100	$1,200	0%
Interest expense	$300	$300	$300	$300	$300	$3,600	1%
NEW LOAN		$1,800			$1,700	$3,500	
TOTAL OP. EXPENSES	$21,050	$23,800	$27,550	$20,550	$23,300	$255,250	54%
PRE-TAX PROFIT (LOSS)	$2,370	($380)	$18,440	($2,620)	$120	$38,600	8%
Fed. taxes	$0	$0	$0	$0	$0	$0	0%
State taxes	$142	($23)	$1,106	($157)	$7	$2,316	0%
PROFIT (LOSS) PRE-TAX	$23,040	$22,660	$41,100	$38,480	$38,600		
NET PROFIT (LOSS)	$2,228	($357)	$17,334	($2,463)	$113	$36,284	8%

Chapter 8
Variance Analysis

Comparing actual to budgeted performance is managing by the numbers in action. The budgets embody your standards. Variance analysis is a process which measures actual performance against those standards.

The process is more easily shown than described. Two variations are shown here, monthly and year-to-date, and shown two ways: based on cash flow and based on P&L. A third variation uses "rolling quarters" in which you add the current month's actual performance to the two previous months' actual performance. This can smooth out month-to-month fluctuations, though this is a refinement you may not feel is necessary. (See **Cash flow monthly variance, Cash flow YTD variance** and **P&L Monthly variance**.)

You choose which budget to follow. Ongoing businesses can ordinarily use P&L-based variance analysis effectively. Most other businesses benefit from the cash-flow budget. If you prepare annual cash-flow pro formas, the cash-flow budget is the best way to control the movement of cash into and out of your business. Ideally you would use the P&L budget to foster profitability and the cash flow budget to ensure liquidity. Steady ongoing businesses can afford to focus on profitability, as their cash flows don't threaten their liquidity. Businesses undergoing change should stress liquidity rather than profitability.

The convenience of using a P&L budget may be the overriding factor. It's better to follow a P&L budget than follow no budget at all.

If you don't prepare monthly cash-flow reports, use the P&L budget approach. Very few small businesses prepare monthly cash-flow reports, though all (or almost all) do watch cash carefully. The important thing is that you have to adhere to your budget, because if you do not, expenses have a horrid habit of creeping up. If you don't at least attempt to follow your budget, there is no point in preparing forecasts or budgets.

Variance analysis is the easiest and most direct of all the managing by the numbers tools. You use your cash flow and P&L budgets to fill in Column C, the projected or budgeted numbers. Then you fill in Column B, actual performance, and finally, calculate the dollar variance, Column D (D = C - B). The percent variation of Column E is calculated by the formula D/C x 100. Sometimes the percent change is more important than the absolute dollar figure.

Cash flow monthly variance

A	B	C	D	E
(Memo sales figures)				
$28,000		$47,000		
	ACTUAL	JAN	VARIANCE	% VAR
CASH INFLOWS				
Cash sales		$15,510		
Cash from receivables		$18,760		
Other		$850		
Total cash from operations		$35,120		
New investment				
New debt				
Sale of fixed assets				
TOTAL CASH INFLOWS		$35,120		
CASH DISBURSEMENTS				
VARIABLE DISBURSEMENTS				
Production costs				
Licensing fees				
Commissions		$5,294		
Contract labor		$470		
Freight		$940		
Total COGS		$6,704		
Travel		$300		
Meals & entertainment		$200		
TOTAL VARIABLE		$7,204		
FIXED DISBURSEMENTS				
Salaries		$7,000		
Payroll taxes		$700		
Benefits		$1,750		
Rent		$1,000		
Utilities		$300		
Insurance		$900		
Marketing & advertising		$7,050		
Professional fees				
Telephone		$600		
Equipment leases		$300		
Repairs & maintenance		$100		
Miscellaneous		$100		
TOTAL FIXED		$19,800		
P & I: Loan 1				
P & I: Loan 2		$450		
Other (describe)				
TOTAL OTHER		$450		
TOTAL CASH DISBURSED		$27,454		
CASH FLOW		$7,666		
CUM. CASH FLOW		$7,666		
OPERATING CASH FLOW		$8,116		
STARTING CASH		$8,500		
+CASH INFLOWS		$35,120		
- CASH DISBURSEMENTS		$27,454		
ENDING CASH POSITION		$16,166		

Cash flow YTD variance

A	B	C	D	E
(Memo sales figures)				
$28,000		$47,000		
	ACTUAL YTD	PROJ YTD	VARIANCE	% VAR
CASH INFLOWS				
Cash sales		$15,510		
Cash from receivables		$18,760		
Other		$850		
Total cash from operations		$35,120		
New investment				
New debt				
Sale of fixed assets				
TOTAL CASH INFLOWS		$35,120		
CASH DISBURSEMENTS				
VARIABLE DISBURSEMENTS				
Production costs				
Licensing fees				
Commissions		$5,294		
Contract labor		$470		
Freight		$940		
Total COGS		$6,704		
Travel		$300		
Meals & entertainment		$200		
TOTAL VARIABLE		$7,204		
FIXED DISBURSEMENTS				
Salaries		$7,000		
Payroll taxes		$700		
Benefits		$1,750		
Rent		$1,000		
Utilities		$300		
Insurance		$900		
Marketing & advertising		$7,050		
Professional fees				
Telephone		$600		
Equipment leases		$300		
Repairs & maintenance		$100		
Miscellaneous		$100		
TOTAL FIXED		$19,800		
P & I: Loan 1				
P & I: Loan 2		$450		
Other (describe)				
TOTAL OTHER		$450		
TOTAL CASH DISBURSED		$27,454		
CASH FLOW		$7,666		
CUM. CASH FLOW		$7,666		
OPERATING CASH FLOW		$8,116		
STARTING CASH		$8,500		
+CASH INFLOWS		$35,120		
- CASH DISBURSEMENTS		$27,454		
ENDING CASH POSITION		$16,166		

P&L monthly variance

A	B	C	D	E
SALES REVENUE	ACTUAL	JAN	VARIANCE	% VAR
Products		$47,000		
Other		$1,000		
Returns & allowances		($150)		
TOTAL REVENUES		$47,850		
COST OF GOODS SOLD				
Production costs		$10,340		
Licensing fees		$3,760		
Commissions		$2,820		
Contract labor		$470		
Freight		$940		
TOTAL COGS		$18,330		
GROSS MARGIN		$29,520		
OPERATING EXPENSES				
Salaries, etc.		$10,000		
Rent & utilities		$1,250		
Insurance		$150		
Marketing & advertising		$7,050		
Travel		$300		
Meals & entertainment		$200		
Professional fees		$200		
Telephone		$600		
Equipment leases		$350		
Repairs & maintenance		$100		
Amortization & depreciation		$300		
Miscellaneous		$100		
Interest expense		$300		
NEW LOAN				
TOTAL OPER. EXPEN.		$20,900		
PRE-TAX PROFIT (LOSS)		$8,620		
Federal taxes		$0		
State taxes		$517		
CUM PROFIT (LOSS) PRETAX		$8,620		
NET PROFIT (LOSS)		$8,103		

P&L YTD variance

A	B	C	D	E
SALES REVENUE	ACTUAL YTD	PROJ YTD	VARIANCE	% VAR
Products		$47,000		
Other		$1,000		
Returns & allowances		($150)		
TOTAL REVENUES		$47,850		
COST OF GOODS SOLD				
Production costs		$10,340		
Licensing fees		$3,760		
Commissions		$2,820		
Contract labor		$470		
Freight		$940		
TOTAL COGS		$18,330		
GROSS MARGIN		$29,520		
OPERATING EXPENSES				
Salaries, etc.		$10,000		
Rent & utilities		$1,250		
Insurance		$150		
Marketing & advertising		$7,050		
Travel		$300		
Meals & entertainment		$200		
Professional fees		$200		
Telephone		$600		
Equipment leases		$350		
Repairs & maintenance		$100		
Amortization & depreciation		$300		
Miscellaneous		$100		
Interest expense		$300		
NEW LOAN				
TOTAL OPER. EXPENSE		$20,900		
PRE-TAX PROFIT (LOSS)		$8,620		
Federal taxes		$0		
State taxes		$517		
CUM PROFIT (LOSS) PRETAX		$8,620		
NET PROFIT (LOSS)		$8,103		

Any variance you consider significant should be investigated. It may be an unpaid bill, or perhaps an unexpected sale. Variances can be good or bad—and in either case, managing by the numbers depends on spotting these variances from the standards.

The monthly variance analysis helps most with short-term variances. Weather can affect sales, utilities and other line items. The goal is to identify and understand the variances, then take action if any action is called for. Sometimes all you want to do is keep an eye on a variance. Variance analysis points out questions for you to ponder.

The year-to-date projections and performance are arrived at by addition. January + February for February, January + February + March for March and so forth.

The year-to-date variance analysis accentuates trends, especially in the dollar variance column. Since small amounts can become large over time, year-to-date is an important part of your analysis. Year-to-date smooths out the inevitable ups and downs. A three-pay-period month, an unusual repair bill, a short spurt in sales can make the monthly numbers look peculiar. Year-to-date figures present a more balanced view of the actual performance of the business.

The main drawback to year-to-date is that it is based on the fiscal year, so for the first few months this smoothing effect is lacking. You can get around this by the "rolling quarters" method. In January, add last November and December actual figures to the January projections. In February, add last December and the projections for January and February. And so on. You can continue this through the year or abandon it once you have the patterns established. This refinement prevents unnecessary worry over temporary blips, especially on the revenue side.

Summary

Variance analysis is a simple and effective tool which provides an easy format to compare your company's actual to its projected performance, both monthly and year-to-date. You should adopt a version of variance analysis to make your budgets effective. Computers have made performing the calculations so simple that there is no reason not to use variance analysis.

Furthermore, it takes only a few seconds to spot variances, and in many cases you will already understand why they appear. The unexpected and subtler variances may indicate that you are doing something very right (or wrong); they help you to latch onto opportunities and blunt threats before it is too late.

Chapter 9
Ratios

Volumes have been written on ratios, but there are really only a handful that matter to most small business owners and managers. With a small set of ratios you can quickly identify where improvements are needed. As you run your business you juggle dozens of variables. Ratio analysis is designed to help you identify those variables which are out of balance.

Bankers and other investors love ratios. This fact alone makes ratio analysis important. If your current, acid test or debt/worth ratio is out of whack with your banker's expectations, money will be imposssible to borrow unless you can explain them.

Ratios are used absolutely, standing on their own as measures of your business at the time the information they are based on was compiled, and relatively, comparing performance to trade or industry standards (RMA and others), to historical performance or to other standards. Both uses are valuable. Keeping track of key ratios over a period of months or years is a powerful way to spot trends in the making.

More subtle uses of ratios are presented in Ch 10, "Strategic Analysis," which pulls all the key ratios together in such a way as to provide specific suggestions for action.

Ratios are commonly categorized in four groups: liquidity, coverage, leverage, and operating.

Keep in mind that all of the following ratios are based on when your financial statements are calculated. This sensitivity to timing is a factor you should take into account. A retail store's balance sheet drawn up just before the Christmas season when inventories are high and accounts receivable are low will present a very different picture than a balance sheet drawn up just after New Year's Day, when inventories will be low and accounts receivable high.

This chapter and the following are based on *Profiting from Financial Statements: A Business Analysis System* (© 1989, The Halcyon Group, Inc., Charleston SC 29412). This use has their full permission.

Liquidity ratios

Liquidity ratios are used to indicate your firm's ability to meet current obligations on time. An illiquid firm has difficulty paying its bills and needs more capital, better management, or both.

The example draws on numbers from Ch 5, Balance sheet example, and Ch 2, Sales by market for last year's sales.

Current ratio = total current assets ÷ total current liabilities

Example: $74,500 ÷ $26,000 = 2.9

The current ratio is commonly used to measure ability to meet short-term debt. The rule of thumb is that this should be at least 2:1. This is because some of the assets involved (especially inventories) may take a while to turn to cash to meet current obligations in a timely way. The current ratio is dependent on the quality of the current assets. This is the most widely used single ratio. Its widespread use highlights the importance of maintaining liquidity.

Acid test or quick ratio = (cash + equivalents + accounts receivable) ÷ total current liabilities

Example: $41,500 ÷ $26,000 = 1.6

This is a more precise measure of current liquidity. The rule of thumb calls for an acid test ratio of 1:1. A ratio lower than 1:1 indicates an unhealthy reliance on inventory or other current assets to meet short-term obligations. A higher acid test ratio may indicate excessive cash or lax collection efforts.

Sales/receivables ratio = net sales ÷ accounts receivable (net)

Example: $356,000 ÷ $33,000 = 10.8

This measures the annual turnover of receivables. Higher values indicate a shorter term between sales and cash collection. Lower values can indicate a collection problem due either to lax collection efforts or low-quality receivables. This ratio is affected by seasonality. If possible, use an average receivables figure rather than year-end.

Days' receivables ratio = 365 ÷ sales/receivable ratio

Example: 365 ÷ 10.8 = 24 days

This measures the average time in days that accounts receivable are outstanding. This ratio is subject to the same caution concerning seasonality. If your terms are net 30, this figure will (or should be) 30 or less.

Cost of sales/inventory ratio = cost of sales ÷ inventory

Example: $356,000 x 38% = $135,000 ÷ $30,000 = 4.5

Use an average inventory figure rather than year-end or a similar unusual figure. The average inventory will give you a truer picture of how your business is doing over the course of the year.

Days' inventory = 365 ÷ cost of sales/inventory ratio

Example: 365 ÷ 4.5 = 81 days' inventory

This ratio is affected by your inventory cycle. It should average 45 days. This is a measure of how you turn your inventories. Higher is generally better, but an abnormally high or low ratio relative to industry figures is a danger sign. Too high a figure is usually caused by either overtrading or inability to maintain adequate inventories, a result of under-capitalization. This ratio doesn't take seasonal fluctuations into account. Cost of sales is used instead of net sales to eliminate imbalances caused by profit margins.

Cost of sales/payables ratio = cost of sales ÷ trade payables

Example: $135,000 ÷ $15,000 = 9

This measures annual turnover of trade payables. Higher values indicate a shorter time between purchase and payment. Generally lower numbers, down to the industry standard, indicate good performance. Below industry standards ("leaning on trade") can indicate liquidity problems. This ratio doesn't take seasonality into account.

Days' payables = 365 ÷ cost of sales/payables

Example: 365 ÷ 9 = 41 days

Sales/working capital ratio = net sales ÷ net working capital

Example: 356 ÷ 49 = 7.3

Working capital is calculated by subtracting current liabilities from current assets. This ratio measures the margin of protection for current creditors and reflects the ability to finance current operations, and also measures how efficiently working capital is employed. A low value indicates inefficient use of working capital, while a high ratio indicates a vulnerable position for creditors.

Coverage ratio

A coverage ratio measures the company's ability to service debt, particularly bank debt. This ratio is looked at closely by bankers and other creditors.

EBIT/interest ratio = earnings before interest and taxes ÷ annual interest expense

Example: $28,500 ÷ $3,500 = 8.1

This ratio measures ability to meet interest payments. In general, a higher ratio indicates a favorable capacity to take on additional debt.

Leverage ratios

Leverage ratios measure exposure to risk and vulnerability to business downturns. The higher the leverage, the higher the risk and the higher the potential profits. These ratios are looked at closely by bankers, especially if the credit is not 100% secured by good collateral. Remember that bankers are by nature averse to risk.

Fixed/worth ratio = net fixed assets ÷ tangible net worth

Example: $22,500 ÷ $51,000 = 0.44

This ratio measures the extent to which owner's equity has been invested in plant and equipment. For creditors, the lower the ratio the better. Note that the assets are net of depreciation and that "tangible net worth" washes intangibles (such as "goodwill") off the books. Substantial leased assets may artificially and deceptively lower this ratio, which has been offered as a specious and potentially dangerous reason to lease plant and equipment rather than to buy it.

Debt/worth ratio = total liabilities ÷ tangible net worth

Example: $46,000 ÷ $51,000 = 0.9

Every banker looks at this measure of the relationship between debt and ownership. High ratios scare creditors, while low ratios may indicate excessive and unprofitable caution. Ask your banker what he or she would like this to be for a firm such as yours. If the answer doesn't make sense to you, explain why your ratio is whatever it is.

Operating ratios

Operating ratios provide a measure of management performance. Comparing these ratios across time is one indicator of efficient management, subject to the usual "all things being equal" reservation.

PBT/net worth % ratio = (profit before taxes ÷ tangible net worth) x 100

Example: ($32,000 ÷ $51,000) x 100 = 63%

This is another ratio where very high or very low numbers indicate possible problems. A high ratio can mean that you are doing a great job. It could also mean that you are undercapitalized. A low value could be the result of overly conservative management of a well-capitalized company. This example indicates possible under-capitalization. In the example (see Ch 4, "Cash Flow"), additional capital of $40,000 was injected. That investment would have lowered this ratio to a more normal 35%, which is high but not dangerous.

PBT/total assets % ratio = (profit before taxes ÷ total assets) x 100

Example: ($32,000 ÷ $97,000) x 100 = 33%

This uses pre-tax profit to eliminate the vagaries of taxation. The higher the better, though it can be distorted by heavily depreciated assets, sizable intangible assets or unusual income or expense items.

Sales/net fixed assets ratio = net sales + net fixed assets

Example: $356,000 + $22,500 = 15.8

This ratio measures the productive use of fixed assets. It also can be used, in conjunction with the next ratio and others, to estimate capital needs and how assets should be allocated in a start-up.

Sales/total assets ratio = net sales + total assets

Example: $356,000 + $97,000 = 3.7

This ratio measures ability to generate sales in relation to total assets. It will be affected by low assets or unusual sales patterns such as a start-up exhibits.

Sales/employee ratio = total sales + employees

Example: $11.5 million + 50 = $230,000

This is a measure of productivity, and is most often used as a comparative measure. A higher figure indicates either better equipment or better personnel management (or both).

Summary
Ratios taken singly can be misleading, but when compared to industry or other norms and followed over time to ascertain trends, they are highly valuable. Ratios help you interpret the relationships of P&L and balance-sheet figures and get maximum information from your financial statements.

Chapter 10
Strategic Analysis

While the preceding chapters will help you spot problem areas in your business, you may wish to delve more deeply into the relationship between ratios, industry or self-derived standards, and workout plans based on these relationships. This is not for everyone. My best advice is to use "fisCAL™" to perform the calculations.

Strategic profit model

The strategic profit model is also known as the DuPont chart. It is a ratio analyzer based on the principle that the most important measure of success of any business is its rate of return on net worth (RORNW). Comparisons of the ratios to either your own or industry standards is important; the variances are an essential component of the model.

RORNW is computed from three ratios:

Net profit margin (NPM) = net profit before tax + net sales

Rate of asset turnover (RATO) = net sales + total assets

Leverage ratio (LR) = total assets + net worth

RORNW = NPM x RATO x LR

If return on net worth is not satisfactory, the source of the problem can be traced quickly through one or more of these ratios, using the strategic profit model. The net profit margin (NPM) is based on the P&L, rate of asset turnover (RATO) is based on the P&L and balance sheet, and the leverage ratio (LR) is based on the balance sheet. By comparing each element of these financial statements to its industry or other standard, the source of low performance can be readily identified.

The strategic profit model for Halcyon's study case, Generic Retail, Inc., is reproduced here.

Strategic profit model

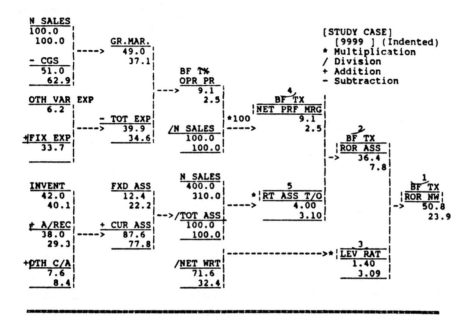

NET WORTH DIAGRAM

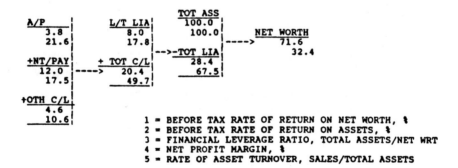

1 = BEFORE TAX RATE OF RETURN ON NET WORTH, %
2 = BEFORE TAX RATE OF RETURN ON ASSETS, %
3 = FINANCIAL LEVERAGE RATIO, TOTAL ASSETS/NET WRT
4 = NET PROFIT MARGIN, %
5 = RATE OF ASSET TURNOVER, SALES/TOTAL ASSETS

The study case data and industry standard data are recorded directly below each account title. Their figures are expressed as percentages of net sales for P&L items and as percentages of total assets for balance sheet items. Thus in the RORNW (furthest right), 50.8 is the study case RORNW, while the industry average is 23.9.

Working backward, from RORNW toward the left, you can trace these numbers back to their source. "fisCAL™" does this automatically. My experience echoes that of other small business owners: I'll do this kind of analysis if I can perform it quickly or have it done for me. Otherwise it gets shunted aside by more immediately pressing items, even though in the long run I know it's more important than today's crisis.

Four levels of analysis are shown in the exhibit on the next page.

The first level looks at RORNW, compares performance to the industry standard and shows the variance from the standard. Performance greater than 110% of standard is reported as "good"; less than 90% as "low," and between 90% and 110% as "satisfactory."

The second level reports identical detail for each of the three component ratios NPM, RATO and LR. Any of these reported as "low" receives a more detailed analysis in the third level.

The third level identifies the specific P&L or balance sheet items that are, compared to the industry standard, responsible for the "low" second-level ratios.

In the fourth level, second-level ratios reported as "satisfactory" or "good" are detailed, together with a checklist of improvement strategies for those ratios that were reported as "low" at the second level.

Schematically:

Level 1
identifies basic problems

Level 2
identifies ratios "responsible"

Level 3
identifies specific accounts which need
to be improved to correct the problems

Level 4
offers additional strategic areas that
may be useful in solving the problems

Strategic profit model action chart

```
              FOR GENERIC RETAIL, INC. STUDY CASE DATED 12/31/00
                     COMPARED TO INDUSTRY STANDARD 9999

========================================================================
1ST LEVEL |                RATE OF RETURN ON NET WORTH
STUDY CASE|                          50.8%
9999      |                          23.9%
% OF STD  |                         212.5%
          |                THIS IS GOOD PERFORMANCE
========================================================================
2ND LEVEL | NET PROFIT MARGIN  |  RATE ASSET T/O    |  LEVERAGE RATIO
STUDY CASE|       9.1          |      4.0           |      1.4
99991     |       2.5          |      3.1           |      3.1
% OF STD  |     364.0%         |    129.0%          |     45.3%
          | GOOD PERFORMANCE   | GOOD PERFORMANCE   | LOW   PERFORMANCE
==========|====================|====================|===================
3RD LEVEL |                    |                    | A/P:  18% STD
          |                    |                    | REQUIRES REVIEW
          |                    |                    |
          |                    |                    |
          |                    |                    |
          |                    |                    |
==========|====================|====================|===================
4TH LEVEL | NT PROF MRG OK BUT: | RT ASS T/O OK BUT: | OTHER FACTORS:
          | TOT EXP: 115% STD   |                    | RENT/OWN DECISIONS
          |                     | A/R: 130% STD      | INVENTORY CONTROL
          |                     |                    | COLLECTIONS
          |                     |                    | PAYABLES CONTROL
          |                     |                    | ECONOMIC ORDER QTY
          |                     |                    | MAKE/BUY DECISIONS
          |                     |                    | DIVIDEND POLICY
          |                     |                    |
          |                     |                    |
          |                     |                    |
          |                     |                    |
========================================================================
```

Gross margin return on inventory investment

FOR GENERIC RETAIL, INC. STUDY CASE DATED 12/31/00
COMPARED TO INDUSTRY STANDARD 9999

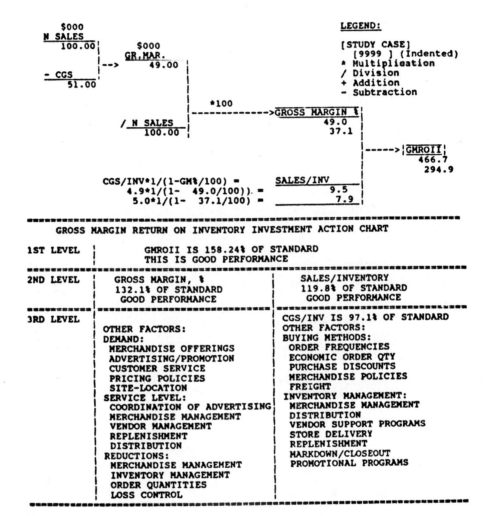

```
$000                                                        LEGEND:
N SALES
  100.00 |     $000                                         [STUDY CASE]
         |   GR.MAR.                                         [9999 ] (Indented)
         |     49.00 |                                       * Multiplication
  - CGS  |--->        |                                      / Division
   51.00 |           |                                       + Addition
         |           |                                       - Subtraction
         |           |        *100
         |           |------------------->GROSS MARGIN %|
 / N SALES|           |                         49.0   |
   100.00 |                                      37.1   |
         |                                              |
         |                                              |----->|GMROII|
         |                                              |       466.7
         |                                              |       294.9
    CGS/INV*1/(1-GM%/100) =       SALES/INV            |
       4.9*1/(1- 49.0/100)). =         9.5             |
       5.0*1/(1- 37.1/100) =          7.9              |
```

GROSS MARGIN RETURN ON INVENTORY INVESTMENT ACTION CHART

1ST LEVEL	GMROII IS 158.24% OF STANDARD THIS IS GOOD PERFORMANCE

	2ND LEVEL	
	GROSS MARGIN, % 132.1% OF STANDARD GOOD PERFORMANCE	SALES/INVENTORY 119.8% OF STANDARD GOOD PERFORMANCE

3RD LEVEL		

	OTHER FACTORS:
	DEMAND:
	  MERCHANDISE OFFERINGS
	  ADVERTISING/PROMOTION
	  CUSTOMER SERVICE
	  PRICING POLICIES
	  SITE-LOCATION
	SERVICE LEVEL:
	  COORDINATION OF ADVERTISING
	  MERCHANDISE MANAGEMENT
	  VENDOR MANAGEMENT
	  REPLENISHMENT
	  DISTRIBUTION
	REDUCTIONS:
	  MERCHANDISE MANAGEMENT
	  INVENTORY MANAGEMENT
	  ORDER QUANTITIES
	  LOSS CONTROL
		CGS/INV IS 97.1% OF STANDARD
		OTHER FACTORS:
		BUYING METHODS:
		  ORDER FREQUENCIES
		  ECONOMIC ORDER QTY
		  PURCHASE DISCOUNTS
		  MERCHANDISE POLICIES
		  FREIGHT
		INVENTORY MANAGEMENT:
		  MERCHANDISE MANAGEMENT
		  DISTRIBUTION
		  VENDOR SUPPORT PROGRAMS
		  STORE DELIVERY
		  REPLENISHMENT
		  MARKDOWN/CLOSEOUT
		  PROMOTIONAL PROGRAMS	

Gross margin return on inventory investment (GMR)

The GMR is similar to the strategic profit model and is used to analyze the performance of a retailer or wholesaler against its most important investment, inventory. GMR is computed from two ratios:

Net profit margin (NPM) = net profit before tax + net sales

Sales/inventory (S/I) = net sales + inventory

GMR = NPM x S/I

The process is the same as in the SPM. If GMR is not showing satisfactory (90% to 110% of standard) performance, you can work backward to find the most likely accounts involved.

The definitions are the same as for SPM. (See exhibit, Gross margin return on inventory investment.)

The first level, GMR on inventory investment, is compared to industry standards. As before, you can use standards derived from your own sources or use more widely available if less specific standards from one of the major databases.

In the second level, the component ratios NPM and S/I are analyzed and compared to industry standards.

In the third level, individual accounts contributing to a "low" second-level report are broken out (if any) and other strategic factors are provided in checklist form.

Index of sustainable growth (g*)

The index of sustainable growth (g*) is used to compute the growth rate of sales that can be sustained from internally generated funds. If your business plan calls for a growth rate higher than its g*, external capital will be needed to fund the growth. As a prudent owner, you will already know that more capital is necessary, but the g* adds a compelling argument.

$$g* = [P(1-D)(1+L)] + [T - P(1-D)(1+L)]$$

where
P = (net profit before tax + net sales) x 100
D = target dividends + profit after tax
L = total liabilities + net worth
T = (total assets + net sales) x 100

If your planned growth rate is greater than your g*, any one or more of the following measures will be required (unless you pare back your growth plans):

• Increase the profit margin by improving buying, manufacturing efficiencies and/or marketing and distribution efficiencies. Since these are goals you are already pursuing, this will serve as a spur to greater efforts.

• Decrease dividends. If you don't pay dividends, consider shrinking your own pay.

• Increase the debt/equity ratio, provided you have the assets and the ability to do this.

• Decrease the total assets/sales ratio by renting, sale/leaseback arrangements and other measures.

Once you have figured these measures' effects on your business' financial shape, recalculate the g*. You may want to revamp your sales growth plans and will certainly have to revise your business plan to accommodate the changes in your perception of what your business can accomplish.

Note that the implied changes affect all of the other elements of the strategic analysis, and you should trace the implications of the changes through another set of RORNW and GMR analyses.

Summary

Budgets, variance analysis, and strategic analysis are specific tools to keep your business on track and answer the tough questions of "How well am I doing against goals, against competition, against trade?" They are powerful tools. Adapt them to your own business's needs.

Note how SPM and GMROI work: they are derived from your financial statements, which in turn come from day-to-day actual performance. By comparing actual performance against standards at each step, you can spot problem areas quickly and take action.

Part II
Individual Measures

The overall performance of your business is built up from the innumerable daily activities performed by you and your employees. The financial statements and daily journals cover some of these activities, but not all, and not even all of the important activities.

The fundamental ideas behind managing by the numbers are that you can control what you can measure and what gets measured gets done.

If you can measure performance, you can manage and improve the results. Your employees want and need to know what they are required to do. Objective measures, agreed to by you and your employees beforehand, are one way to convey such knowledge. More important, knowing what they are required to do helps improve their performance. Most of us like to know whether or not we are doing a good job and seek feedback, which we use to improve our performance. This doesn't mean that we are all Stakhanovites (after the eponymous hero of Soviet labor, a Stalinist John Henry), but I'd argue that the evidence clearly shows that employees prefer to do a good job if they know what "doing a good job" involves.

Other employees, the ones we'd rather not have, can be encouraged to change or sometimes frightened away by the imposition of clearly objective measurable performance standards. In the unhappy event that you have to fire someone, a paper trail documenting failure to meet agreed-upon minimum performance standards goes a long way toward defusing potential legal claims.

Any process can be measured. Processes range from planning to manufacturing to delivering the product. Quality is a measure of the effectiveness of the manufacturing process or, by extension, of the sales process if you understand customer satisfaction as a quality issue. Some examples will be presented in following sections – but your ability to select the right measures for your business is key.

Deciding what to measure and how to measure it is not always easy. Fortunately, help is available. Just about every aspect of human behavior has been studied, measured, analyzed and argued over by generations of intelligent people. Business is no exception. Within your trade association you can find more ways to measure what you do than you will ever use.

The problem is discipline. Several years ago when we were faced with a sales slump I knew perfectly well that standard, objective measures of sales performance would help turn the slump around. Number of prospecting calls and letters, number of cold calls per week, number of presentations or proposals made, number of contacts needed to close a sale, number and profitability of sales all help pinpoint where a sales problem is rooted. That's all well and good—but I failed to require that such data be kept. I knew what was needed, didn't demand it, was very unhappy with the results and could only blame myself.

This is by no means uncommon, especially when dealing with sales personnel who are afraid of their performance being measured. Their usual cries are "Every situation is different," "No two customers are alike," "It's the economy, not me," and so on. As a result, the real problem (Where's the problem in the sales funnel and how can we correct it?) gets lost in a hubbub of personalities and defensive posturing.

Measuring individual performance works. It delivers results. Employees like having clearly defined goals more than having vague "do better" demands (or no demands at all) placed upon them. Employers like it because it makes communications clearer and profits higher and replaces personality clashes with sharply defined, measurable performance standards that are either met or are not met. The results are no room to hide, no room to twist away from responsibility, no room for excuses.

It does require work. Finding the key measures for individuals and processes takes savvy and research. Keeping track takes constant effort. Some employees will resist keeping accurate records, and a few may falsify records. Try getting salespeople to file call reports if they aren't used to them! But over the long haul, managing by the numbers pays off in dollars, self-esteem and job satisfaction.

Chapter 11
Everything Can Be Measured: Villaume's Universal Form

Henry Villaume's "Universal Form" is an ingenious and inspired tool to help you measure just about everything. Mr. Villaume, who is an engineer and management consultant with years of experience helping small business owners turn their businesses around, says he's not sure just where the Universal Form comes from, but it is in widespread use. My paraphrase of Mr. Villaume's explanation of how to use the form follows. If there are confusions, they are my fault; Mr. Villaume's own explanation is wonderfully clear.

The first side has a faint graph, 10 x 10-inch with half-inch accent lines. This side is used for rough written notes, scaled sketches and diagrams. It is especially helpful in roughing out layouts and finding interfaces, and in graphing data to show or highlight desired relationships. The 10 x 10 format lends itself to graphing dollars or percentages.

The power of managing by the numbers is attained in part by using numbers to communicate progress or performance to your employees. If your immediate goal is to reduce returns, for example, you might plot sales and returns on a weekly basis, posting the chart where everyone will see it. Prattling about improved quality and the importance of doing things right the first time is less effective than showing, via a graph, progress toward reduced returns. The graph helps spark interest in maintaining and improving performance, in part by providing direct visual feedback.

See **graph 1**. Weekly rejects are plotted for each of three assembly teams. The graph reveals more than progress; note that in week 10 all teams lost ground. This could be due to supplier problems, internal problems, weather or a complex assortment of factors. That would be up to management to determine; quality is a management problem.

Graphing helps make the numbers come alive. You can use this form to track ratios: see **graph 2**. Or sales. Or profitability. Or whatever you wish. Most people find it easier to look at a trend line than columns of numbers. By keeping the graphs simple and directive, you can help your employees help you attain your goals.

Villaume graph 1

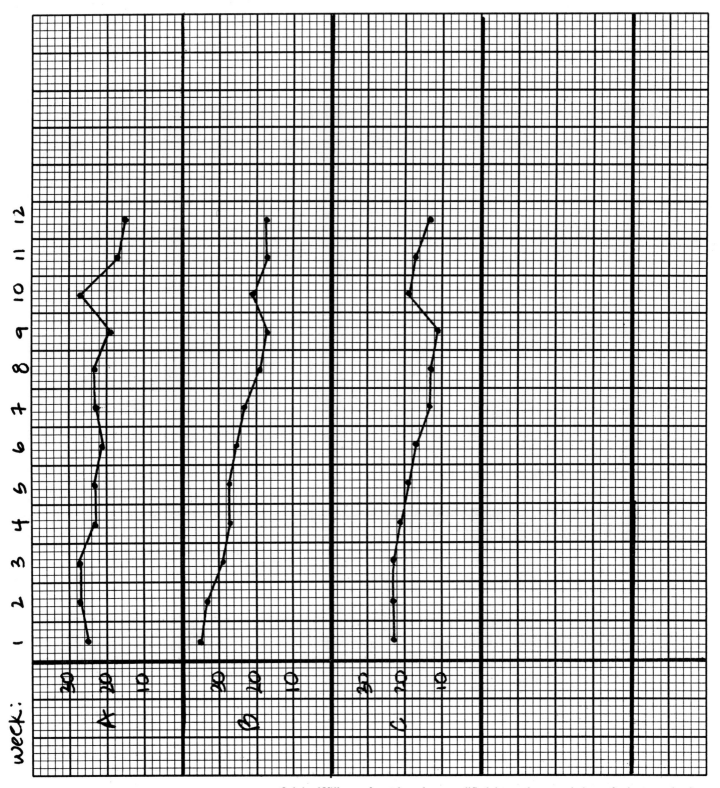

Original Villaume forms have been modified due to the constrictions of print reproduction.

Villaume graph 2

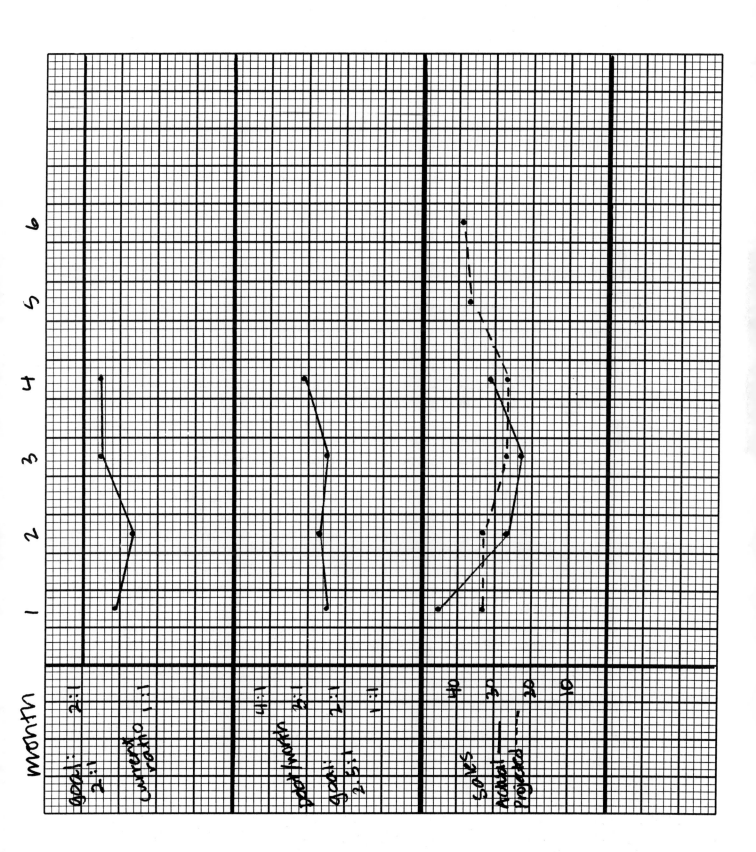

Side two is a spreadsheet, with 16 columns and 32 lines below the three header lines. Accents are provided every fifth line.

"This side is sometimes referred to as the Universal Planning Sheet and resembles the old green spreadsheet we grew up on, with the one major advantage that it is 8 1/2 x 11 in size," Mr. Villaume writes. "In this, the day of the computerized spreadsheet, you may (with some justification) question the value of such a sheet. This is, however, an ideal sheet to plan out a new computer spreadsheet by defining column heads, sizes, logical order and so forth. It does provide a most convenient self-organizing format for data being collected to study some problem away from the location of a computer.

"Enclosed are some headings (see **graph 3**) that have been developed to forcefully and directly communicate particular job expectations to an employee. Where such forms have been utilized, genuine misunderstandings have been eliminated and marginal performers converted to star performers because they more clearly understood management expectations.

"The convenient numbering to 31 in the first column allows a single sheet to report the performance daily for an entire month, with weekly and monthly totals for an entire year on 12 sheets of paper. How very convenient for review times and to track individual professional performance. Very constructive guidance or coaching can be provided from such records.

"This form is so universally helpful in the organization of information that it would be impossible to list all of the possibilities here. The only limitation in the usefulness of this form is truly the creativeness of the user."

As Mr. Villaume notes, the Universal Form can analyze everything people do, by day or whatever period you select. The financial uses are important, but it is in the realm of people-monitoring that it is most impressive. Suppose you are managing a group of telemarketers. You want to track objective factors such as the number of calls made, sales by product lines and dollar totals. If you are new to such a sales process, you want some further information: How many calls does it take to get a sale? What lists are effective? Which script works best? When is the best time to call? The information has to be gathered and analyzed and the Universal Form is well suited to the task. See **graph 4.**

Over a very few days, you will establish ratios and learn which scripts, lists, times and so forth apply to your business. You can then use the data as a standard by which to measure individual performance on a daily basis. If you know that it takes 10 calls to make one sale, you can focus your efforts on identifying ways to help your telemarketers reach their goals—and know with a reasonable degree of certainty where problems in attaining their goals originate.

The diagram makes the trends of key indices pop out at you. Some manufacturers use this form for daily or even hourly reports, especially if they run more than one shift. Your imagination is the boundary. You could follow output and downtime for each machine, station or operator, track defects and measure them against your known norms. Thus you could get to the root of a production problem within a day or even less.

Villaume graph 3

For month of:

	7-11	11-3	6-9	kitchen	waitress		Food	Bar	hrs/meal (kitchen)/waitress)		
	1	2	3	4	5	6	7	8	9	10	11	12

Restaurant Manager

Day	Bkfst # $	lunch # $	dinner # $	hrs	hrs/meal #	hrs	hrs/meal #	$	$			
1 M weather, etc.												
2 T												
3 W												
4 Th												
5 F												

Telemarketer

6 Remarks	calls out	cont-acts made	% success	order taken	$ total	$ order	calls in	service order #	$ total	$ order	Product spiff Lines 1,2,3
7											
8											
9											
10											

Inside Sales Rep

11 Remarks	calls in	calls out	total calls	# orders taken	# items total	$	# items b/o	$ total order	% items shipped	%	$ in 50%
12											
13											
14											
15											

Marketing Sales Manager

16 Remarks	RFQ #in #out	Quotes won $	Quotes		Sales calls by Sales Force				Plant visits		
17			NE	SE	SW	WC	MW	NW			
18											
19											
20											

Accounts Payable Clerk

21 Remarks	invoices rec'd	Processed - validated - matched	Posted $	Inv. value paid	$ value	Age Prox calls in out	hrs/ invoice				
22											
23											
24											
25											
26											
27											
28											
29											
30											
31											

Villaume graph 4

Telemarketing

	calls out	contacts made	% success	# of orders	$ total	$ per order	Products ordered A	B	C	D		
Remarks	1	2	3	4	5	6	7	8	9	10	11	12
1 Script A												
2 9-11 AM												
3 11-1 PM												
4 1-3 PM												
5 3-5 PM												
6 5-7 PM												
7												
8												
9												
10												
11 Script B												
12 9-11												
13 11-1												
14 1-3												
15 3-5												
16 5-7												
17												
18												
19												
20												
21 Script C												
22 9-11												
23 11-1												
24 1-3												
25 3-5												
26 5-7												
27												
28												
29												
30												
31												

Villaume graph 5 (side 1)

Cash management

		week 1		week 2		week 3		week 4				
		1	2	3	4	5	6	7	8	9	10	11	12
1	Cash in bank		3000		2000	1100		3100					
2	cash inflow												
3	cash outflow												
4													
5	Bookings (6-12)		25000	35000		30000		25000					
6	Shipments (4-8)												
7	A/R 0-30												
8	31-60												
9	60+												
10													
11	A/P 0-30												
12	31-60												
13	60+												
14													
15	Payroll												
16													
17													
18													
19													
20													
21													
22													
23													
24													
25													
26													
27													
28													
29													
30													
31													

Villaume graph 5 (side 2)

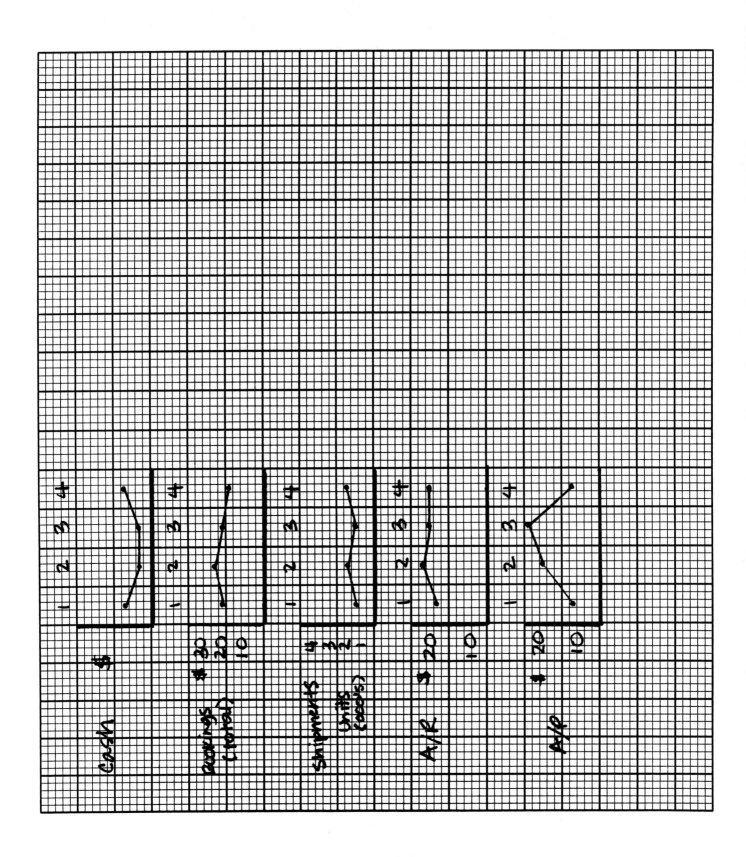

For an example of financial management, see **graph 5**. The Universal Form is nothing if not flexible; Mr. Villaume recommends monitoring some financial measures both numerically and graphically. After all, he claims, "If I know where I am every week, no month is a surprise." Of course you have to determine what you wish to track in your business. A one-page form such as this (or John Blackford's) keeps you from drowning in a sea of numbers or flood of paper.

The general rule: determine what to measure, then keep it simple. The Universal Form will help you do this.

Chapter 12
Sales and Marketing Measures

Sales drive your business. If you can understand and measure the sales process, from pricing and promotion through after-sales service, your prospects for profit are propitious. Leave them to chance and you invite disaster.

Assuming you have made all reasonable efforts to fit your products to your market's demands, the most nettlesome aspects of sales and marketing are (not necessarily in order) pricing, measuring the effects of promotional efforts (advertising, public relations, and in-house or point-of-purchase) and monitoring the efforts of your sales force. These are slippery subjects.

Pricing

For most of us, there is surprisingly little latitude in the prices we can charge. Few businesses are immune to price competition. While there are good reasons to seek alternatives to price competition, price competition always depresses prices, whether you join in or not. True, you can offer better service, better delivery, more convenient financing to justify higher prices—but competition will dampen price increases and tends to establish an upper limit to what the market will accept. Don't enter into price competition if you can possibly avoid it. You won't be able to underprice a Walton's or a Kmart; they will swamp you. An inviolable rule: Small businesses cannot afford to be the low-cost providers.

Ask what is the least you can charge and still survive? This can be roughly established by referring back to your break-even points (see Ch 6), estimating the probable number of units you will sell at various prices, and matching the results against your break-even points (preferably keeping profit as a fixed expense). Since

$$\text{Price x unit sales} = \text{revenue}$$

you need to look at both price and unit sales. In an ideal world, you'd look for the price which maximizes revenue. In the real world, where you face competition for constantly changing markets, prices will fluctuate. So rather than try to add a preset margin to each product, you do better to know what the competition is charging, what your cost structures are so you don't undermine yourself, and to keep a very close watch on inventories and market demand.

All of this boils down to common sense. If you watch your costs, matching a competitor's prices may be a profitable strategy. If your costs are higher than theirs, matching prices will harm you or force you to adopt non-price strategies.

Establishing prices

1. Establish your break-even points, treating profit as a fixed expense to be conservative and provide a margin for unanticipated problems.

2. Convert the break-even point to unit sales. As noted above, price x unit sales = revenue. In your sales forecast you broke sales into product lines; use that as the basis for this step. Some product lines are less price-sensitive than others, and you presumably know which of your lines are more (or less) price-sensitive. You can get very technical in this kind of reasoning, but the more complex, the less apt the procedure is to be used. Better rely on your own sense of the market, checked by your employees (especially sales employees). The question to raise is "What will this price change do to sales?" A lower price may lead to higher volume, but if a small price increase leads to a large sales volume drop, it is a price-sensitive item. You can do some experimenting with prices yourself or (better) get this information from your trade association.

3. Check the competition. Shopping the competition is helpful for many reasons: you find what works for them and what doesn't, gain ideas about improving your own business, get a sense of what your competition is up to. The Villaume Universal Form can be used to track prices:

Competition	Aug	Oct	Dec	
Store 1				
Product A				
B				
C				
D				
E				
Store 1				
Product A				
B				
C				
D				
E				

While you don't want to be purely reactive in pricing, competitors' pricing strategies affect yours. Try to keep it simple (key products or services only) and keep the information up to date. How often you check is up to you. It depends on what business you're in.

4. The expected contribution (revenue minus direct cost) is another key factor. Ask yourself what effect different prices will have on the contribution to your P&L or cash flow. In the chart below
  Revenue = price x unit sales
  Total cost = unit cost x unit sales
  Contribution = revenue - total cost

Product/Service	Price	Unit sales	Revenue	Unit cost	Total cost	Contribution
Product 1	$10.00	150	$1,500	$2.00	$300	$1,200
	$9.00	175	$1,575	$2.00	$350	$1,225
	$11.00	135	$1,485	$2.00	$270	$1,215
	$12.00	125	$1,500	$2.00	$250	$1,250
Product 2	$19.95	1000	$19,950	$2.37	$2,370	$17,580
	$21.95	600	$13,170	$2.37	$1,422	$11,748
	$18.95	1100	$20,845	$2.37	$2,607	$18,238
Product 3	$2,500.00	200	$500,000	$650.00	$130,000	$370,000
	$3,000.00	150	$450,000	$650.00	$97,500	$352,500
	$2,000.00	300	$600,000	$650.00	$195,000	$405,000

What else is involved? Considerations of handling, shipping, installation and other post-sales service can change your pricing decision. You cannot ignore them. It may be more profitable to sell fewer units at a higher price. You must know all the cost factors that affect your business, and factor them into your pricing strategies.

5. By far the most important considerations are the marketing implications. Pricing has more to do with perceived value to the customer and prospect as with any objective or intrinsic value. A diamond is a lump of carbon. A Chevy will get you there just as quickly as a Rolls Royce. Several retailers mentioned a "formula" to me:

Perceived value = perceived benefits x price

("Formula" because it doesn't work mathematically. Perceived benefits and prices are so intertwined that it is not possible to separate them. A lowered price often results in lowered perceived value.)

The wisdom in this formula is that as you increase prices you also have to increase perceived benefits to the purchaser lest you erode the perceived value.

On the other hand., you can cheapen a product's perceived value by pricing it too low. Several years ago I tried selling a newsletter program to Chase Manhattan Bank for what I thought was a reasonable $1,200 a year. I got nowhere. When I mentioned my failures to an experienced and perceptive friend, Jim Howard, he responded by telling me to go back and ask for $12,000 a year. I did so and returned with a contract. "Lack of courage in pricing," Jim said, "is the biggest small business marketing problem."

Jim's point is worth thinking about. Price changes affect all of your projections and financial statements, to say nothing of your profits. Yet many small-business owners still think that low prices are the best way to attract customers. Keep in mind that lowering prices is easier than raising them.

If there is one moral to be drawn from this brief discussion of pricing, it is to guard your margins. You have to have that gross margin to meet your profit goals. Price is one component of the complex of factors that affects your gross margin. If you know the costs involved, you'll make better pricing decisions.

Measuring the effectiveness of promotions is another vexed area. John Wanamaker said that 50 cents of every dollar he spent on advertising was wasted, but he didn't know which 50 cents it was. If we can measure the impact of our promotional dollars, we should be able to use those dollars more wisely.

The occasional "You can't measure advertising" counter-argument is a straw man. The effectiveness of advertising is tied to increased sales (measurable), increased store traffic or inquiries (measurable), or even something as tenuous as increased awareness of your business. This too can be measured.

All promotions and advertising programs need objective measurable goals. These may be so many new customers, or inquiries, or trials of a product (or whatever). If you have no goals for the promotion, you won't be able to know if the promotion works. Set time limits: ten new customers in 10 days, 400 inquiries by the end of the month, 15,000 samples distributed in Milwaukee by January 10th. The basic managing by the numbers rules apply: set objectives, measure performance, modify and proceed. The improvement of effectiveness over time will amply repay the effort involved.

You can measure the results of most promotions. It isn't always easy, nor 100% accurate, but you can keep track of increases in traffic, inquiries and sales and form a sense of the relation between promotions and such increases. Ask your advertising agency. If they can't help you measure results, be leery. If you can't measure the results, you can't manage the promotion.

Direct mail is a good model for focusing the effectiveness of your promotions, even if you don't use direct mail. The promotion has costs you can accurately determine in advance (postage, print, creative charges and so on), results which come in somewhat later and a clear positive or negative impact on profits. If the promotion meets its goals, you repeat it. If not, modify it, test it again and repeat the process.

Direct mail is easily tracked. You send out so many letters, catalogues or brochures and receive responses. Track these on a daily basis and you quickly learn what lists and offers work for you.

There are other objective ways to determine the effectiveness of promotions and advertisements.

Ask customers: where they heard of your business, why they buy from you rather than your competition, where they are from. This kind of survey can be informal but you have to keep track. Write down their responses, compare the results to other surveys.

Track sales patterns. These tend to be stable over time for non-seasonal businesses and for the sales season in seasonal ones. You need to know the basic pattern so you can locate the anomalies, the sales or traffic surges that follow your promotions. If you advertise and get an unusual burst of sales, you know the advertisement worked.

Ongoing advertising programs are, if effective, reflected in increased market share and sales. If a major competitor suddenly emerges, you'll know it. But otherwise, standard measures work. For example, coded dollars-off coupons give you a fix on which newspaper works best for your business. The cost of ongoing advertising is necessary. Trim the budget at your peril.

Measuring Promotions

1. Set measurable goals for each promotion. You might aim for identifiable sales of advertised items, increased foot traffic, number of inquiries, gain in market share, or a host of other measures. Just saying you want to maintain business or increase it some doesn't do. The more specific the goal the more targeted the promotion will be—and that saves a lot of money by itself.

2. Measure the results. This becomes easier to do over time, once you establish acceptable and expected goals. The first few attempts may be inconclusive, particularly if you haven't formed the habit of seeking goals before advertising.

3. Repeat the process. Testing one variable at a time may work; at other times radical change may be more appropriate. That depends on your situation and judgment. Marketing consultants can help you establish testing procedures.

Painless call reporting

One of the major problems in managing salespeople revolves around preparing and submitting call reports. Management wants to know what's going on, in part to ensure as far as possible that sales levels are OK, in part to find ways to improve sales levels. Salespeople balk. The normal call reports are viewed as a waste of time, if not worse, and as a result are not done. Or done partially. Or faked.

The typical call report requires a lot of needless duplication (names, address, telephone and FAX numbers and so forth) and does nothing to further the new communication that might reveal the true activity pattern at a given account. The form shown on the next page, courtesy of Mr. Villaume, addresses this problem directly by making the form report from 15 to 30 individual actions after being headed by a clerk or a computer. The salesperson reports dates and actions only.

Management gains a chronological activity chart that clearly monitors progress toward the goal of a major sale or just reports routine servicing of the account, depending on what is appropriate. Periodic copies provide an up-to-date file for management to control the account through any transitions.

The salesperson gains valuable time without giving up the organizational support of a good background file and follow-up system. The tracking columns are headed by the oft-preached primary steps towards making a sale (from prospecting and qualifying through post-sales support). This serves a dual purpose: it helps you and your salespeople spot the places in the sales funnel where the going is difficult and serves as an ongoing reminder of what to do next and when to do it. By tracking the checkoffs from top left to bottom right (generally southeast, as Mr. Villaume says), a quick scan reveals how the account is progressing.

Call form

Customer Jolly Envelope & Padding Co.

Background Data
1426 Lafferin.
Hysteria, ME 04963

Jack Jolly, GM
(207) 681-2401

Jane Fear, PA
(207) 681-2405

FAX
(207) 681-2409

Contacts Bill to Shipping Headquarters.

Activity Date	Describe Activity	Prospecting	Qualifying	Needs/Solution	Establish Commitment	Propose	Close	Support	$ Quote	$ Sale	Activity Code	Follow-Up Date
2/26	Visit Jack + Jane re form padding							✓			✓	2/28
2/28	Phone Jane re quote qty 3/9									690	C	3/10
3/9	Jane - where is job?										P	ASAP
	- shipped late PM										C	3/12
3/12	Jane - did work arrive? OK? yes.										C	3/12

Sales Volume

Month	1989	1990	1991
O		1482	
N		1690	
D		1437	
J		3741	
F		New 2920	
M		200	
A		292	
M		630	
J		1400	
J		3279	
A		2864	
S		1940	

As with other forms, modify it to your needs. I like it as it stands. If I had known about this form several years back, I'd have avoided some severe sales problems.

While this form goes well beyond managing by the numbers, it filters some critically important information. It shows sales volume for each account for three years by month so it helps identify sales patterns for each individual account. Trends up or down are easy to spot. By examining the activity report, some specific ideas of how to deal with a slump are shown. Suppose a contact leaves the account and the salesman has to identify and qualify a new contact in the organization. The checkmarks back up, necessary steps are taken and the account (you hope) becomes reactivated.

Much of this information is buried in more complex reporting systems and is therefore of little use. As an unfortunate consequence, many salespeople rely on anecdotes and the most current (if fleeting and misleading) impressions of their accounts. At the very least, you as the manager need to understand and be able to quantify the sales funnel.

Managing by the numbers requires more than vague answers about the sales process. You'll find these forms help you gather information to provide precise answers about amounts, dates and other important facts. Among the questions you need answers to are the following:
• How many prospects do you need to get one sale?
• How long does it take to turn a prospect into an account?
• How many phone calls, visits and other contacts are involved in the average sale?
• How large is the average initial sale? Follow-on sale?
• What are the most common sticking points in the sales funnel and when do they occur?
• What are the buying patterns of the average account?
• How many people—and their titles, if appropriate—are involved at each account?

Filling these forms out is not arduous. Filing the form is simplicity itself: photocopy it. The salesperson keeps the original. This provides an ongoing record of account activity.

Summary

Managing by the numbers applies to all aspects of the sales and marketing process, or can be adapted to it. Since sales drive every business, it is feckless at best to leave critically important aspects to chance or fallible memory. Simplify the reporting process so you can gather the objective information to make decisions more profitably.

Chapter 13
Quality, Productivity and Personnel

A common gripe about quality and productivity improvement programs is that it's swell to aim for no defects or to use statistical quality control methods, but that in real practice it's too difficult to implement such programs over a period of months, especially in small companies.

One method is to keep track of quality problems by charting them, display the chart (updated frequently) prominently, and invite your employees to help solve their own problems. You can think of this as a 95% solution. (The extra effort required to attain a 100% solution goes well beyond the bounds of this book.) If nothing else, it keeps attention directed toward the quality problem. If the rate of rejects increases, the reasoning goes, the sooner you spot it the better. The quality problem needn't be a production problem. Customer complaints about service, delivery or courtesy are also quality concerns.

The suggested approach is:

• Keep a record of all complaints. Most of the complaints will sort themselves out into a few categories which will be familiar to you. We find that delivery problems are among our most common and intractable problems.

• Set goals. "Reduce late shipments to no more than five per month" might be a place to start. "No late shipments" may be our ultimate goal, but we want to have goals that are realistic.

• Monitor and chart progress weekly. This is arbitrary; it could be daily or monthly. How many shipments? When? What carriers? The idea is to correct a problem, not lay blame. The objective record helps keep people on track, as well as providing background information for performance evaluations.

• Constantly seek improvements. If something gets out late, how come? How can we prevent it in the future? Small ideas cumulatively have a big impact.

A similar approach helps with productivity problems. Mr. Villaume's Universal Form is useful for gathering the information. (See **Output analysis, station 1.**)

Output analysis, station 1

Output Analysis : Station 1

DAY	Hour 1	2	3	4	5	6	7	8	9	10	Daily Total 11	Cum. Total 12
1 Mon	setup	setup	40	42	40	40	42	45			249	249
2 Tues	setup	10	41	40	44	54	45	45			270	519
3 Wed	40	40	40	40	42	40	38	down	down		280	799
4 Thurs	Down	Down	setup	43	45	47	45	45	46	42	313	1112
5 Fri	41	39	42	44	54	49	50	48	clean		358	1470
6 –												
7 –												
8 Mon												
9 Tues												
10 Wed												
11 Thurs												
12 Fri												
13 –												
14 –												
15 Mon												
16 Tues												
17 Wed												
18 Thurs												
19 Fri												
20 –												
21 –												
22 Mon												
23 Tues												
24 Wed												
25 Thurs												
26 Fri												
27 –												
28 –												
29 Mon												
30 Tues												
31 Wed												

Suppose your interest is in output, setup and downtime. Keep track of each machine daily, hourly, or other. The chart on the preceding page is an example. You first establish hourly and shift norms. Then monitor performance to make sure that performance is up to these norms. If not, you can quickly spot the variance and take corrective action as necessary.

The beauty of such objective records is that they provide standards or norms which help your employees improve their performance (and thus your performance as well). Without such objective standards, there is no way to feel good about each day's performance. Norms function the same way batting averages do. It's natural to want to know what's expected of you. One of the major complaints about small business owners and managers is that we don't let our employees know what's expected of them, so any evaluation is understandably viewed as arbitrary.

Managing by the numbers for other purposes

The routine for establishing norms varies from one business to another, from one employee to another, but the general approach is the same.

1. Ask yourself and your employees: what results do we want? Then start by paying attention to them. Managing by the numbers begins with goal-setting. If you know what results you want, you can then work backward to where you are now and determine the steps necessary to reach those goals. A few examples of desired results:

Clerical jobs
• no mistakes (or no more than ten per week)
• answer phone within three rings every time
• report to all inquiries within one working day
• no stationery or postage stockouts

Production worker
• minimum 275 units per shift
• under one percent error rate
• machine downtime two hours per week or less
• improve setup time from one hour to 45 minutes by the end of December

Copywriter
• meet all deadlines on schedule
• submit 25 headlines for each ad

These are measurable, objective standards. By tracking actual performance, baseline norms can be set, then discussed with and by the concerned employees. Managing by the numbers works best when the norms or standards are arrived at by both management and employees. You may find that your employees will set standards that are unrealistically high. You want the standards to be high enough to be worth pursuing, but low enough to be attainable. Otherwise disillusion and discouragement set in.

2. Meet with the individual employee, explain your goals for the business, ask how they can help meet them. This may involve more than you expect. Do they need more or newer equipment? training? better lighting or better work-floor layout? more or less supervision?

3. Ask them what measures apply to their jobs as they see their jobs. You've had your say already. The objective measures best suited to each job will come from joint efforts. As the owner or manager, you have to coordinate their job with your goals, but that's another matter.

4. Once the norms are agreed upon, measure and monitor actual performance. Encourage and praise as needed.

Make the measurements come alive by presenting them in chart or graph form. If performance is sub-par for a reason, fine. What's the reason? If performance is above par, fine. What's being done better or faster than expected? Your employees want to do a good job, and one of your duties is to provide them with objective, "good job" measures.

Chapter 14
Measuring Management

As mayor of New York, Ed Koch gained a measure of fame for running around asking people on the street, "How am I doing?" Like many of us who manage enterprises, he wasn't sure how good a job he was doing. Feedback was important to him. He didn't want to wait for the next election to find that the voters thought he was doing a lousy job.

Same with us. If we see "the bottom line" as our only measure of job performance, the feedback will be too far removed from our daily activities. What can we do? Most of us know what we should do, if only vaguely. We must plan ahead, schedule, coordinate, monitor and control. We must keep costs down, sales and profits up.

Some measures of management effectiveness come straight off the monthly financial statements:

- Profit, both for the month and year to date, compared with projected monthly and year-to-date profit.
- Gross margin, monthly and year to date. Most of your operating expenses are fixed. Credit or discredit for keeping to fixed expenses is a good measure of the office manager's performance (or whoever is responsible), but not so good for the general manager's performance.
- Net sales, monthly and year to date.
- Cash position, measured by current and acid-test ratios.
- "Bankability" measures, especially the debt/worth ratio.

These are objective measures. Managerial compensation is frequently tied to them. If you are the owner, the value of your business is directly affected by these measures.

If your business has been slumping due to external conditions, or if your business is a start-up or in transition, trends in these measures are good indices of performance. Ongoing businesses track trends also, but their managers are expected to maintain the measures, which is a somewhat different task from "begin to approach" or "make progress toward" the numbers.

In a fast-growth business, track management of cash and available credit. The danger is illiquidity, so concentration on cash flow is necessary. Gross margin as a percentage of sales is crucial. One danger in fast-growth is that the variable costs lurch out of control. Keeping an eye on gross margin is one way to measure control over variable expenses.

Some non-financial measures are good indicators of how well you're doing as a manager. They are somewhat idiosyncratic, but objective. As an example, for a book-publishing company:

President
• prepare business plan for the September board meeting, including updated financials
• meet with each employee twice a year (performance and salary evaluations)
• secure financing needed to support business goals by January.

Managerial measures will be less precise than those for office or factory employees, as duties are wider and less regulated. But their measures are no less objective. Business plans are or are not ready on the stated date. Financing is or is not in place on time. Performance evaluations are or are not performed. And so on.

Editor
• publish 12 new titles in time for the next publishing season
• sign 24 contracts for new titles for next year's list
• revise 6 titles from backlist
• prepare editorial budget by September.

Marketing manager
• prepare weekly news releases
• prepare six newsletters (every other month)
• attend eight trade shows
• prepare an advertising and marketing budget
• prepare and substantiate next year's sales forecast by September
• meet sales objective from business plan

All of these are objective measures, yes or no, on time or not, which help people measure their progress. Accountability works best when the measures are clearly stated and easily measured. Complex measures take too long. You can set schedules (six new titles signed by May, six more by August) to bring the long-term down to manageable size, or leave it to your executives. They know what has to be done (assuming you've done your job), and know what happens if they don't reach these goals.

Summary

As you form the habit of setting goals and standards based on your business in its economic and market context, managing by the numbers becomes easier. It isn't a panacea but rather a handy and helpful tool. Its focus on goals makes managing by the numbers forward looking; the comparison of actual to projected performance provides a good measure of progress. Measuring progress towards a goal makes attaining those goals easier. Each time you review progress you'll have another chance to think through your strategies, find the sticky points and devise ways to overcome them.

For individuals, managing by the numbers permits and encourages self-motivation. Give your employees measurable goals, provide a measurement system, and stick with it until your employees have gone through a few weeks of monitoring their own progress. You'll be delighted with the results.

Appendix
Selecting an Accountant

Unless you've been trained as an accountant and have considerable experience, to decide what to track and what to ignore is too important to try to do yourself. The false economy of doing it yourself is highly dangerous. While doing it yourself may appear to be a way to save much-needed cash, it isn't. You won't get the kind of information you need, you won't get accurate information, and what you do get won't be timely enough to make your managerial tasks easier.

There are some shortcuts you can take to keep your accounting bills to a sensible minimum. The more precise your questions to your accountant can be, the lower the bill.

Start by seeking trade information. What do businesses in your field keep track of? How do they keep on top of their information needs? If you can, get sample financial statements from businesses like yours. Your trade association can provide samples and will be able to steer you to sources of very specific financial information ranging from seminars and study groups to consultants specializing in your kind of business.

Ask the following questions of some local business owners who have more experience than you:

• Are you happy with the information you now get?
• How would you improve your information systems?
• How often do you look at your financials: weekly, monthly or quarterly?
• What does your accountant help you with?
• Does he or she help with pricing decisions?
• What are the key financial items you follow? Gross sales, gross margins, operating expenses, cash balance?
• What non-financial information do you keep track of? Examples might be number of items kept in stock, unit shipments, number of sales calls made or daily customer counts. These kinds of information can be very valuable, especially if you are relatively new to the business.

• If you could only have three pieces of information, what would they be? Many business owners insist on keeping ongoing track of sales revenue, gross margin and profit or loss. Manufacturers track billings, bookings and backlog.

• Do you use a computer? If you do, are you happy with your accounting package? (And what is it?)

Details differ from business to business, but the financial structure businesses like yours have in common is the best starting point. The details make a huge difference, but will evolve as you go along. One way to look at this is that the financial skeletons are very similar, but the flesh that goes on those bones will vary dramatically, depending on the age and stage of the business.

Basic business activities are the same for all businesses: buying and selling. There are no exceptions. You have to keep track of sales and expenses. You have to keep track of what you own and what you owe. You have to maintain sufficient records to keep the IRS from getting cross. The IRS conducts free seminars to help small business owners comply with regulations. These range from acquiring a proper IRS identification number to payment schedules for withholding taxes, FICA taxes and other obligations.

Depending on the state, county and city your business is located in, you will have sales, income and other taxes to pay. Your insurance agent can alert you to mandatory insurance coverages such as unemployment and worker's compensation.

The more of this basic information you can gather the better. It will allow your accountant to get right to work on your behalf, rather than spending his or her time scouting up industry-specific formats and information that you could have found in your spare time.

The mechanics of bookkeeping and record-keeping are important. You need consistency and accuracy, which in turn demand that the mechanics be simple and direct. Complicated systems don't work; they get in the way. To assure a clean flow of information, some common-sense precautions apply:

• Keep written records. Nobody has a memory keen enough to track all the transactions a business undergoes.

• Use a checkbook for all disbursements. "Petty cash" accounts tend to be overused in small businesses and lead to unnecessary waste as well as a woeful lack of information. Money dribbles away. The discipline of writing a check mysteriously cuts costs. It also provides a record of what was spent, when.

• Use technology. Electronic cash registers and scanners are worth the investment, since they provide a track of receipts and help you manage inventory. If you find that businesses like yours usually use computers, scanners or other technologies, take it as a hint. Use sales books, including duplicate sales receipts.

The time these tools save pays the investment in them off fast. They are inexpensive insurance against pilferage and fraud; records have a deterrent effect on the light-fingered.

Why hire an accountant?

If you don't know why you need an accountant, you're too naïve to be in business. If you can't afford to pay for an accountant, you're undercapitalized and won't survive for long.

Why hire an accountant? For the financial management and tax expertise they bring to your business. Accountants are trained to set up your books, gather data and reshape it into highly formatted financial statements, and then draw judgments from the information. A good accountant will help you deal with bankers and other investors and suggest the right kinds of controls and economies. They know a lot about how to finance a business and smooth out cash flows.

Good accountants quickly develop a sensitivity to the needs of the small businesses they work with. They can and will draw attention to drawbacks in your financial plans. This hold-back function is extremely important for most of us entrepreneurs, blinded by our enthusiasm to the pitfalls in our plans. This role of devil's advocate is invaluable.

Taxes are the least important reason to hire a capable accountant. The role of the accountant is to help you get the information you need, when you need it, in a form that enables you to make better decisions. This doesn't mean that the role of your accountant in minimizing your tax liabilities is unimportant. Your main job is to make a profit so you have to pay taxes, and you should run your business accordingly. Tax considerations affect profitability but are secondary to the main purpose.

Some business owners hire one accountant for tax purposes and another for managerial reasons. Although this is extreme and too expensive for most small businesses, the skills required in tax work are not the same as required in helping you run your business more efficiently. A common complaint about accountants is that they look backwards not toward future events, and are in some instances little more than expensive bookkeepers. You wouldn't turn to your accountant for advice on an aggressive growth strategy, though you should ask his or her advice on whether you can afford that growth, and if not, what your options might be.

Accountants come in various degrees

Certified Public Accountants (CPAs) are the most professional, with credentials based on education and experience. They are expensive and may not be necessary for your business. Many small businesses get along just fine with public accountants or with "business counselors" affiliated with franchises such as General Business Service. While these accountants and advisors are not as credentialed as CPAs, they may be just as expert in small business matters. Or more so: some CPA firms are uneasy in dealing with small businesses, and major CPA firms (regional or national) won't put their most experienced hands to work on your problems. Instead, you'll get the newest boy or girl on the block. (The same applies to bankers, incidentally. Small business owners, who need experienced bankers the most, get the least experienced.) More than one small business owner complains that they spend too much time training new accountants.

Public accountants and business counselors are apt to specialize in small businesses, make their living from helping them grow and prosper and tend to remain with local firms. By concentrating on small business, they learn the quirks and whims of running small, undercapitalized companies, acquire a depth of small business financial knowledge that is deeper and more detailed than a Big Six accounting firm junior accountant, and become founts of knowledge about local conditions. The tradeoffs (there are always tradeoffs, unfortunately) are that these accountants and counselors aren't as well versed in tax minutia, don't have the big banking and financial connections of CPAs and may be less sophisticated than you might wish.

The most frequent reason to hire a CPA, whether independent or a member of an accounting firm, is that only CPAs can audit your books. This can be important for bankers and other investors. On the other hand, most small businesses do not have to provide audited statements, and the substantial added expense of audited statements can be avoided. However, the comfort factor that CPAs afford bankers, even if they give a qualified opinion rather than an audit, may be worth the added cost.

You have to get along with your accountant. You need a financial advisor you can level with and whose opinions you can trust. If you want some point more fully explained or are worried about the business, an accountant can be a good friend to have. If you are putting together a financing proposal, you need someone who can tell you whether the numbers hang together. As with any professional, you need the unvarnished truth.

How do you go about finding the right accountant for your business? If you already have an accountant and are not sure that you are getting the service you deserve, act as if you were new in town. You aren't obligated to stay with an accountant if you don't wish to. You want to find a number of apparently qualified accountants (CPAs, PAs or business counselors), then choose from this pool of qualified professionals.

- Speak with other business owners. Ask them who they recommend, what problems they have with their accountants and what questions to ask when interviewing accountants.
- Ask your banker. Most bankers keep a list of accountants they feel comfortable recommending to small business owners.
- Check with your vendors. They tend to know who the good professionals are in your area.
- Use local business groups such as the Chamber of Commerce as a preliminary screen.
- Once you have a list of three or more accountants who seem to meet your needs, call on them. Make appointments, tell them what you are looking for and what you think you might need to spend.

When you interview accountants, remember that they are in business too. Just as you wouldn't hire a doctor purely on cost comparisons, don't hire an accountant just because he's the cheapest in town. Sometimes that's an expensive way to go. Some of the questions to ask your prospective accountants include:

- Have you worked with businesses like mine before? If not, are you willing to learn about my kind of business?
- Can you put me in touch with some of your clients? Some of your ex-clients?
- What are your charges?
- Do you charge a retainer or do you bill only for work performed?
- If you don't think you'd be the right accountant or firm for me, could you recommend some accountants who might be right?

When you check their references, ask

- How responsive are they?
- Do you get reports and filings on time?

• How well do they work with you?
• Can they help with banking relationships?
• Do you feel you can level with them?
• Would you recommend that I hire them?

Setting up the books

Do not reinvent the wheel. Or the information system. Do your research, ask questions, keep notes and let your accountant set up your books and recommend the most appropriate accounting method for your business.

What information do you need? Most small businesses can be run with three monthly statements (balance sheet, cash flow pro forma, and profit & loss). Some businesses need information more often. Some retailers want daily sales and customer count information, which they use to compare with previous years on a day-to-day basis.

Just learning what information you can use is a major undertaking. If you are experienced in your kind of business, you may or may not know what information you need; it may make sense for you to do what a beginner would do: ask. Start with trade sources, including the trade association magazines and newsletters, editors and consultants to the trade and other experts. The costs will be trivial compared to the savings in accounting charges. Different businesses have different information needs. The most successful businesses in your line are the ones who know what information they need and when they need it. Emulate them, at least until you have better ideas.

If you can, get copies of other businesses' charts of accounts. The chart of accounts forms the backbone of your general ledger, which in turn is the core of your accounting system. Whether you use a simple pegboard system or a sophisticated computerized system, you need a chart of accounts that meets your financial information needs. Your accountant will have ideas of what he would like you to have, not necessarily tailored to your information needs. If you tell him what you want to keep track of, and why, and what you may want to track in the future, your books can be set up to make the information available.

Choosing the right accounting system is difficult. You can't make the decision purely on the basis of cost: While a box full of receipts and bills and cancelled checks may be cheap, it certainly isn't cost effective.

The simplest acceptable small business accounting systems are the pegboard or one-write systems sold by Safeguard, General Business Services and others. These rely on two basic journals, the cash disbursement and the sales & cash receipts. These work very simply. The cash disbursement journal uses checks with a carbon strip, so you write the check and at the same time make a copy on the journal. Hence the name "one-write." The journal itself has numerous columns (Safeguard has 33) to distribute the check into the appropriate accounts, plus ample space to describe miscellaneous items. Your accountant will help you choose which accounts (from your chart of accounts) to use. Ask your accountant if a one-write system would work for you.

The sales & cash receipt journal is similar. Daily entries are made to these journals, then at the end of the month the information is summarized and transferred to the general ledger. Ledger cards for accounts payable, accounts receivable, inventories and purchases complete the system.

These one-writes are simple, easy to use and for most small businesses are more than adequate for keeping track of the day-to-day operations and generating financial statements.

Double-entry and traditional accounting systems

Some businesses have to be on an accrual system as opposed to a cash system. These companies will either have to make numerous adjusting entries to a one-write or adopt a double-entry system. The difference between a cash system and an accrual system is that in a cash system, revenues and expenses are booked when cash changes hands: a merchant sells a shirt for $24 and books a sale of $24 the same day. In an accrual system, there is often a lag between when the sale is booked and when payment is received. A magazine publisher sells a one-year subscription and receives $24 today, but books the sale in 12 increments of $2 per month, which has the effect of deferring income.

Manual double-entry bookkeeping systems have worked just fine for years and are the model for both one-write and computerized systems.

The structure of double-entry systems is deceptively simple: Total debits must equal total credits. Journal entries are made daily recording all transactions the company is engaged in: sales and cash receipts, purchases and other disbursements. These transactions are compiled in general ledgers monthly. Adjusting entries to cover matters such as depreciation and amortization, reduction of loan principal, dividends and changes in net worth are made at the end of each month before the books are closed. The balance sheet and P&L are built on the information contained in the general ledger. At the end of the year or other accounting period, the accounts are summarized and balanced and the cycle begins again.

Some economic historians maintain that the invention of double-entry bookkeeping had as great an impact on history as the invention of the printing press. If the accounts don't exactly balance, an error has been made and can be quickly located without reconstructing the entire set of books. This is the standard against which the other systems are based. Your accountant will be thoroughly familiar with the ins and outs of this kind of manual system and will help you understand the flow of information through it. You do not have to become an accountant to use and understand it.

Computerize?

You may have more transactions than can easily be handled by a full double-entry manual bookkeeping system. Fortunately, packaged computerized accounting systems are more adaptable, less expensive and more reliable than ever.

The advantages of computerized systems are speed, ability to handle sizable amounts of data and, best of all, the ability to pull a balance sheet, P&L or cash flow at any time. The drawbacks are the vulnerability of such systems (unless you carefully make backups of data) and the time it takes to learn the ins and outs of the systems.

If you can use a one-write system or have only a small number of accrual accounts, there are several computerized programs (including "one-write plus™") which are mirror images of the simple pegboard systems.

If you have more complex needs, there are specialized programs for many industries, as well as some more general packages that may be adapted to your needs. Unfortunately, most software sellers have only the foggiest notion of what goes into an accounting package, so you may have to find a specialist VAR (Value Added Reseller) to help you install the system you choose and then train you or your bookkeeper in how to run it.

A word of caution: Not all accountants are computer literate, and very few of them are prepared to install systems and train operators. To gain an appreciation and understanding of computerized accounting packages, talk with people who are already using them. They can tell you, more clearly than anyone else, what they like and dislike about their packages. Computer user groups such as the Boston Computer Society (BCS) are another excellent source of unbiased information. If you are planning to computerize, the BCS is a wonderful bargain. Call them at 617–367–8080 for details.

Bibliography

Always start your research by taking your librarian to lunch. A good research librarian will save you a lot of time and worry. Ask him or her what is available to help you find information specific to your industry first. There's a lot out there.

Almanac of Business and Industrial Financial Ratios, Prentice-Hall. Check your library for this one.

Complete Guide to Finance and Accounting for Nonfinancial Managers, Stephen A. Finkler, Prentice-Hall, 1983. A broad introduction to general finance and accounting topics. Very good on applying analytic techniques to management decisions, avoids analysis paralysis, good explanation of how and why the numbers lead to better decision making.

Complete Guide to Starting a Used Bookstore, 2nd ed., Dale L. Gilbert, Upstart Publishing Company, 1986. The best "how-to" book I've read. Funny, trenchant, occasionally obscure but always interesting.

Financial Control for the Small Business, Michael M. Coltman, ISC Press,1982.

Financial Control for the Small Business, F. Leslie Coventry, Jordan & Sons, UK, 1982.

Financial Management for Small Business, E. Rausch, AMACOM, 1982.

Financial Management of the Small Firm, 2nd ed., Walker & Petty, Prentice-Hall,1986.

Financial Studies of the Small Business, 10th ed.,1987, Financial Research Associates (510 Avenue J, S.E., PO Box 7708, Winter Haven FL 33883–7708.) Key balance sheet and P&L information, key ratios, five-year trends for small businesses. Used in Halcyon's fisCAL™ database, this is a key source.

Financial Tools for Small Business Management, DeThomas & Dereiter, Oasis Press.

Financial Tools for Small Business, Cary, Omer and Olson, Prentice-Hall, 1983.

Forecasting Sales and Planning Profits, Kenneth L. Marino, Probus Publishing, 1986. Excellent. The MP–SR (market potential–sales requirement) gives two looks at forecasting sales that, taken together, strengthen your forecasting skills. Strongly recommended.

How to Organize and Operate a Small Business, 8th ed., Clifford M. Baumback, Prentice-Hall, 1988. Excellent textbook, the standard others aim at.

Robert Morris Associates Annual Statement Studies, published annually by Robert Morris Associates (RMA), 1616 Philadelphia National Bank Building, Philadelphia PA 19107. The bankers' Bible. Contains an excellent description of key ratios and their applications, used by banks the world over. Especially good for larger businesses, but some applicability to smaller enterprises.

Small Business Financing, American Bankers, 1980.

Maximizing Cash Flow: Practical finance control for your business, Ronald Press, 1986.

Small Business Reporter, Bank of America (Dept. 3120, PO Box 37000, San Francisco CA 94137). The Bank of America has a long history of helping small business. This superb series of pamphlets ($5 apiece) covers a range of general management topics (marketing, finance, etc.) as well as some specific businesses and professional practices. Well worth getting their catalogue.

Small Business Sourcebook, 3rd ed., Charity Ann Dorgan, ed., Gale Research, 1989, 3 volumes. The best single source of live and print information for over 200 specific small businesses. Provides a detailed listing of similar sources for the small business community in general.

Sweat Equity, Geoffrey N. Smith and Paul B. Brown, Simon & Schuster, 1986. Fascinating anecdotes about high-growth, high-profit companies. Contains excellent ideas on spotting opportunities, marketing, and keeping a company vibrant. I especially enjoyed the segment on PawPrints: how to maintain margins and farm out production.

Index